Living at Hartrigg Oaks

Living at Hartrigg Oaks

Residents' views of the UK's first continuing care retirement community

Karen Croucher, Nicholas Pleace and Mark Bevan

The **Joseph Rowntree Foundation** has supported this project as part of its programme of research and innovative development projects, which it hopes will be of value to policy makers, practitioners and service users. The facts presented and views expressed in this report are, however, those of the authors and not necessarily those of the Foundation.

Joseph Rowntree Foundation
The Homestead
40 Water End
York YO30 6WP
Website: www.jrf.org.uk

ISBN 1 85935 132 8   (paperback)
ISBN 1 85935 133 6   (pdf: available at www.jrf.org.uk)

Cover design by Adkins Design

Cover photograph of Hartrigg Oaks by Peter Smith Photography

Prepared and printed by:
York Publishing Services Ltd
64 Hallfield Road
Layerthorpe
York YO31 7ZQ
Tel: 01904 430033; Fax: 01904 430868; Website: www.yps-publishing.co.uk

Further copies of this report, or any other JRF publication, can be obtained either from the JRF website (www.jrf.org.uk/bookshop/) or from our distributor, York Publishing Services Ltd, at the above address.

Contents

List of tables and figures

Tables

Figures

Acknowledgements

Many people have participated in this research project. We have greatly valued all their various contributions.

The research team are grateful for support from the Joseph Rowntree Foundation, which made this research project possible. We should particularly like to thank Janet Lewis and Michael Sturge for their encouragement and enthusiasm throughout the research.

We received great assistance from the residents of Hartrigg Oaks who gave up their time to complete questionnaires and to participate in interview and discussions. Without their help and co-operation, the research could not have taken place, and we should like to thank everyone in the community.

We should also like to thank the staff of Hartrigg Oaks who gave up their time to be interviewed, and assisted us in various ways throughout the evaluation. Our particular thanks go to John Kennedy, Karen Pendlebury and also to Rachel Plues, who supported the research during the time that she worked at Hartrigg Oaks.

The help of other local service providers in York who participated in the research was much appreciated. Our thanks also go to the New Earswick Residents' Forum for their help with the research.

We should also like to thank the participants in the Hartrigg Oaks Monitoring and Evaluation Advisory Group, who included: Janet Lewis, Cedric Dennis, Des Les Grys, Chris Vellenoworth, Dianne Willcocks, Rachel Plues, Rena Fenteman, Margaret Barnet, Rosalind Priestman, Tony Dale, Dr Christine Oldman, Michael Sturge, Don Brand, Alyson Pollock, Paul Johnson and William Laing.

Karen Croucher
Nicholas Pleace
Mark Bevan
Centre for Housing Policy, University of York
www.york.ac.uk/chp/

1 Introduction

Britain is an ageing society. Between 1961 and 2001 there was an increase in the population aged 65 and over of 51 per cent, with 9.4 million people being aged 65 and over at the time of the 2001 Census. The 2001 Census also shows that there will be more people aged 65 and over than are aged under 16 by 2014 as the average lifespan continues to increase (Source: Office of National Statistics). Family and social networks are also changing. More people will live alone in later life as divorce rates rise and family relationships become more complex and more distant (Scales and Scase, 2000).

At the same time 'age' is being redefined. People in their fifties and sixties no longer see themselves as 'old', and retirement is seen as a rewarding and active part of life. Concepts of age are emerging which reject the notion of older people being a 'burden' on society and which embrace ideas such as the third age, the grey pound and greater empowerment of older people. The diversity of older people's aspirations, expectations and needs has now been recognised (Department of Health, 2001).

Housing need in later life can no longer simply be equated with a need for care and support, as this fails to recognise the wide-ranging housing needs and preferences of older people. Traditional models of sheltered housing and very sheltered housing are being replaced, in part because they were unable to provide the care and support some older people needed to avoid an unwanted move into residential care and in part because of their failure to recognise the diversity of housing need in later life (Butler *et al.*, 1981; Neill *et al.*, 1988; Oldman, 1990; Sinclair and Williams, 1990).

Innovative models of housing for older people have emerged, such as 'flexible' or 'extra care' housing in both the social rented and private sectors. These models aim to accommodate both 'fit' and 'frail' older people, providing socially supportive, stimulating environments in which older people may live wholly independently, and also receive extensive care and support services when required (Hasler and Page, 1998; Oldman, 2000). Rather than simply focusing on care and support, these models address a range of needs: quality of accommodation; opportunities for social networking; affordability; and enablement of independence. These new models are the focus of considerable interest among policy makers, as evidenced by the drive to encourage new forms of supported housing, such as 'extra care' schemes, within the Supporting People programme (Office of the Deputy Prime Minister – ODPM, 2003).

Here, we report research on Hartrigg Oaks, one of these innovative new models of housing and care for later life – the first British example of a continuing care retirement community (CCRC). Hartrigg Oaks offers a combination of high-quality accommodation, communal facilities, care services and flexible financial arrangements, which is intended to allow residents to lead active and independent lives without uncertainty and fear about how future care needs will be met or paid for. The scheme is financially self-sufficient and non-profit making; no Government subsidy or charitable funds were provided to assist with its development.

The research was concerned primarily with the views and perceptions of the residents of Hartrigg Oaks. It addressed two key questions:

- What attracted residents to Hartrigg Oaks?

- How well did Hartrigg Oaks meet the needs and expectation of its residents?

Beyond these questions, the research also sought to review any lessons that might be applied to the possible replication of the Hartrigg Oaks model.

The research was carried out between 2000 and 2002. Both quantitative and qualitative methodologies were employed in two sets of fieldwork conducted in 2000 and 2002, which included a resident survey, focus groups and face-to-face interviews. The research methods are discussed in Appendix A.

Drawing on both European and North American CCRC models, Hartrigg Oaks was developed on a greenfield site in York by the Joseph Rowntree Housing Trust (JRHT) at a capital cost of £18 million. The development of Hartrigg Oaks has been documented by Rugg (1999), and a description of Hartrigg Oaks can be found in Sturge (2000). An overview of Hartrigg Oaks can be found at: http://www.jrf.org.uk/housingandcare/hartriggoaks/

Hartrigg Oaks is designed to allow older people to live independent lives in their own homes, with a range of care and support services available as and when needed. There are three main elements to Hartrigg Oaks, which covers a 21-acre site:

- One hundred and fifty-two bungalows to which domestic help, emotional support and care services can be delivered

- 'The Oaks Centre', around which the bungalows are clustered, which houses communal facilities and acts as a base for care and support services delivered to the bungalows

- 'The Oaks Care Centre', generally referred to as 'The Oaks', a 42-bed registered care home, providing short stay, interim and permanent residential care for bungalow residents.

The bungalows are built to Lifetime Homes[1] specifications, making them suitable for wheelchair users and relatively easy to convert should adaptations be necessary. The bungalows are significantly larger than typical retirement community accommodation, and they each have a small garden and an allocated parking space.

The Oaks Centre contains a coffee shop and restaurant, meeting rooms for residents, a library, arts and crafts facilities and a health activity centre incorporating a gym and spa pool. There is also a small shop, hairdressing salon and minibus for resident use. Resident-led groups and activities are actively encouraged. The Oaks is located in the same complex.

The minimum age at which someone can move to Hartrigg Oaks is 60. By 2002, there were 206 residents. One-third of the population had a partner, the remainder being single or widowed. Women outnumbered men by a ratio of 2:1, and the average age of the community, as at 1 January 2003, was 78.

Continuing care retirement communities like Hartrigg Oaks are largely financed through an insurance-based model. Residents pay a capital sum on entry and an annual fee. These funds are used by a CCRC to create a pool for funding care and support services on which any resident can draw. Continuing care retirement communities are designed to function on the basis that the majority of their residents at any given point in time are contributing to this pool, rather than drawing care and support from it. This financial model allows a CCRC to guarantee its residents that their annual fee will not increase according to the amount of care and support they use, as all residents contribute equally and can draw equally from the pooled resources of the scheme.

Two important implications arise from this financial model. The first is that a CCRC must be careful to ensure that it has the right 'balance' of residents because, if too many residents draw on care and support at any one time, a scheme could theoretically be bankrupted (Rugg, 1999). As a consequence, all potential residents are asked to undergo a health check when they apply to live at Hartrigg Oaks. The second is that a CCRC must offer housing for later life that appeals to older people who anticipate living independently for at least several more years. The financial model depends on there being a majority of younger and fitter residents who pay into the CCRC, but who do not make many demands on its care and support services.

At Hartrigg Oaks, the capital fee (Residence Fee) and the annual charge (Community Fee) can be paid in several ways. There are three types of Residence Fee:

- a 'fully refundable' fee, which can be refunded, without interest, to the resident (or their estate)

- a smaller 'non-refundable' fee

- an 'annualised' monthly payment, rather than a one-off capital sum.

There are two main types of Community Fee:

- the flat-rate 'standard fee', which covers service charges and any care or support that a resident requires (including permanent residential care)

- the 'fee for care' arrangement, whereby a resident pays a lower annual service charge only, but has to meet the costs of any use of care and support services themselves.

On 1 January 2002, 71 per cent of residents were paying the standard fee. Those residents who were living as couples, or sharing a bungalow, paid a reduced Community Fee on the basis that they provide each other with some elements of support. As at 1 January 2002, 24 per cent of residents were 'fee for care'.[2]

Standard fees were around £5,000 per annum, and the initial Residence Fee was around £100,000, during the period of the research. The JRHT estimated that approximately 25 per cent of older people in the UK would have sufficient capital and/or income to allow them to enter a CCRC with charges like those of Hartrigg Oaks.[3]

This report first addresses the question of what it was that attracted residents to Hartrigg Oaks in the first instance (Chapter 2). It then moves on to consider what aspects of life in a CCRC were the most fulfilling or challenging for residents, what facilities were most appreciated and valued by residents, and to explore the reasons for differing levels of satisfaction (Chapter 3). The view of residents of the spectrum of care, the needs assessment procedures and ways in which care is delivered are then considered (Chapter 4). Finally, we discuss some of the implications of the evidence that has come from this research (Chapter 5).

Appendix B contains a monitoring and statistical report prepared by the JRHT from its own management information on Hartrigg Oaks. These data were collected in parallel with the research and were not drawn upon by the University of York team. Appendix B provides useful information on the day-to-day operation of Hartrigg Oaks, covering resident characteristics, care and support services, use of residential care and further information on the financing of Hartrigg Oaks.

2 Moving to Hartrigg Oaks

Drawing on the qualitative and quantitative data collated during the project, the research examined in some detail residents' reasons for moving to Hartrigg Oaks. It is clear that the decision was complex and mediated by a range of factors. For most, as well as probably being the last major housing decision that they would make, becoming a Hartrigg Oaks resident also involved a major financial investment and a change in lifestyle. This chapter examines the motivations of those who chose to become residents of Hartrigg Oaks.

Applying to live at Hartrigg Oaks

To become resident at Hartrigg Oaks an individual or household must first pass the health and financial checks. However, when Hartrigg Oaks first began to seek residents, there was an element of uncertainty about what the health status of prospective residents should be. The CCRC model was new in the UK and, while there was a need to ensure a balance of 'fit' and 'frail' people within Hartrigg Oaks, there was also a concern to ensure the community got up and running as soon as possible. This led to the admission criteria being less strictly applied during the early operation of Hartrigg Oaks than was to be the case later on. Reflecting management's and residents' concerns that the community had initially been slightly unbalanced, there is now a greater emphasis on ensuring a high proportion of residents have reasonable health status. Priority in allocation of vacancies is now given to younger applicants.

Bungalow residents' reasons for moving to Hartrigg Oaks

Reasons for leaving last home

Most of the first bungalow residents moved into Hartrigg Oaks over 1998–99. The 2000 survey of bungalow residents drew the majority of its respondents from this group.[1] Figure 1 presents some findings about the reasons why bungalow residents had left their last home.

While 'health worries' were not a particularly prominent reason for leaving their last home, people had clearly been thinking of their health when they reported not wanting to put pressure on their families to look after them (shown as 'not pressure family') and in expressing a wish to 'stay independent'. Some reported that their previous home or garden had become too much for them to manage (shown as 'old garden too much' and 'old home too much' in Figure 1).

Figure 1 Bungalow residents' reasons for leaving their last home (by percentage of residents)

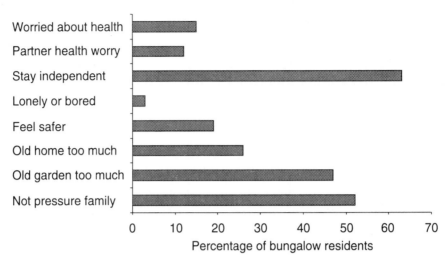

Source: 2000 Postal Survey. Base: 177 residents

Prior to moving to Hartrigg Oaks, almost all the bungalow residents had lived in their own home, the majority of them for more than a decade (72 per cent). Forty per cent had previously been residents of York, and another 31 per cent had been residents of North Yorkshire. Ten per cent had come from London and the South East, with the remainder coming from other parts of England, Scotland and Wales and a few returning to the UK from overseas.

The 2000 and 2002 interviews with bungalow residents emphasised that a fear of becoming dependent and isolated, particularly when living some distance from family, or in a rural area, had been an important factor in deciding to move to Hartrigg Oaks. In the same way, being no longer able to drive, or being worried that it would eventually be difficult to continue driving, played an important role in the decision of some people to move to Hartrigg Oaks.

> I had a vision of myself as an elderly lady who couldn't go out, sitting and waiting for someone to come and dress me and feed me, and I didn't like the idea at all.

> ... our daughter was 60 miles away and our son about 120 miles away and we realised that if anything happened then we couldn't possibly depend on them for help.

The interviews also re-emphasised the importance to some residents of not putting pressure on their children or other relatives. This was particularly noticeable when someone had cared for an older relative and was unwilling to put their own family through a similar experience.

Well, it was peace of mind really, we both had parents who lived in their own homes too long … it was alright while you were there, but when you closed the door you didn't know what had happened behind that door, so you had that worry and it was with you all the time. And [husband] and I decided that our children were not going to have that, so that was one of the reasons that made us look around for something on these lines.

In respect of their worries about isolation and not wanting to pressure children, the bungalow residents at Hartrigg Oaks had similar motivations to those found in other studies that have examined the reasons for housing moves in later life. However, there was one important difference. Hartrigg Oaks residents had generally been *anticipating* the implications of a deterioration in health, whereas older people moving into sheltered housing and similar settings tend to be moving on the basis that their health status actually has deteriorated (Appleton, 2002; Hanson, 2001; Oldman, 1990; Tinker *et al.*, 1995).

Moves to Hartrigg Oaks could, in contrast, often be described as 'preparatory moves' that were designed to maintain independence on the assumption that independence would be undermined were someone to stay in their existing home.

Fear of crime was a much less important factor in deciding to move than it was for older people moving to social rented sheltered housing schemes (ODPM, 2001). This may reflect a tendency of Hartrigg Oaks bungalow residents previously to have lived in relatively low crime areas.

Bungalow residents' reasons for choosing Hartrigg Oaks

Some bungalow residents had considered other housing options before choosing Hartrigg Oaks. Just under one-quarter had considered buying a smaller home than their existing one (23 per cent), and one-fifth had looked at buying private-sector sheltered housing (19 per cent). Ten per cent reported having looked at 'similar' retirement communities to Hartrigg Oaks. Many other options, such as staying with relatives or arranging care services at home, had been considered by small numbers of residents.

Most residents had, however, only considered Hartrigg Oaks itself (57 per cent). In interview, it became clear that many residents had not been actively considering any options for later life until they had heard of Hartrigg Oaks. Some had become interested when they heard of the scheme through friends or relatives, and others had called in to see the development simply out of curiosity as they lived locally.

Many bungalow residents viewed the alternatives to Hartrigg Oaks in quite negative terms. Hartrigg Oaks itself was seen by a high proportion of interviewees as the best alternative available to them.

It's what so many of us want. You don't want to move into a home where your every action is controlled, where you just sit around with a lot of other people in their old age doing nothing in particular, until your therapist comes to give you a little I don't know what. I've seen homes like that, we all have, and it's very depressing. But here you are your own woman, man, couple, whatever. You can come and go as you please, you have complete independence, and yet there are communal activities if you want friendship, and there is this eventual promise of care until you die.

Had I written my own specification of what I would like to have, the Rowntree Trust had produced it for me, it covered all the points, particularly for a person living on their own …

Figure 2 summarises the main reasons given by bungalow residents as to why they had chosen to move to Hartrigg Oaks.

The major attractions of Hartrigg Oaks were the quality of the bungalows and the extensive care services that were available on site. The physical location of the site was also important to many residents in their choice to move there, as was its geographical position in York. Half of bungalow residents reported being attracted by the JRF name. Similar numbers reported being attracted by the fee packages offered

Figure 2 What attracted you to Hartrigg Oaks? (by percentage of bungalow residents)

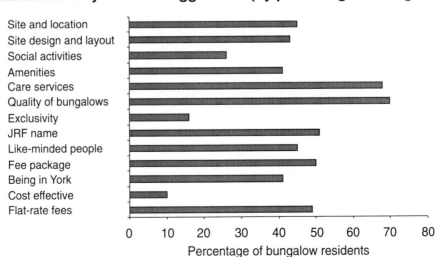

Source: 2000 Postal Survey Base: 177 residents

by Hartrigg Oaks and by the 'flat-rate fees' which, if they opted for the standard Community Fee, would not increase regardless of their use of care services. A smaller number saw Hartrigg Oaks as the most cost-efficient alternative for providing for themselves in later life. The amenities offered by Hartrigg Oaks were another attraction for a substantial number of residents. One-quarter of bungalow residents also reported being drawn to the social activities on offer. Almost half of the residents were attracted by the prospect of being with like-minded people. It was notable that, among the quarter of bungalow residents who were Quakers, 76 per cent reported being attracted by the presence of 'like-minded people'. Smaller numbers of residents reported being attracted by the 'exclusive environment' (shown as 'Exclusivity') at Hartrigg Oaks.

There were some variations between different age groups.

- People over 80 were more likely to emphasise the care services being on site and less likely to cite other factors.

- People aged under 70 were more likely to emphasise the amenities, social activities and location of Hartrigg Oaks; however, they were no less likely to refer to care services than people aged over 80, showing the importance of 'preparatory' moves.

- People living with their partners were less likely than those without a partner to mention social activities as a reason for moving to Hartrigg Oaks (16 per cent compared with 35 per cent).

- Women were more likely than men to mention social activities as a reason for choosing Hartrigg Oaks, which may have been explained in part by their also being significantly more likely to be living alone (women outnumbered men two to one at Hartrigg Oaks).

The bungalows

> As soon as we saw the show house we were sold straight away, without actually having thought previously of moving …

Many residents reported having been attracted by the build quality and space standards of the bungalows. The generous space standards allowed them to retain precious possessions, while the option in many bungalows to convert the loft space into another room allowed them to have relatives to stay, or gave them more room for work and hobbies. Importantly, the size and design of the bungalows were reported by many residents as giving them the sense that the bungalows were a 'proper home', offering the same independence and privacy as their previous homes. The site layout, with its closes of bungalows with their own small gardens and clear boundaries, also reinforced this feeling that Hartrigg Oaks offered a house in a community that could become a home, not a space in an 'institutional' setting.

> I didn't think of it as sheltered accommodation for myself. I wouldn't have moved into one of those, but I didn't want to move twice, and I saw this very much as what I wanted because it was like living in my own house.

Continuing care

Preparatory moves, made in anticipation that health status and the ability to live independently would diminish as age increased, were centrally important in explaining why older people chose to move to Hartrigg Oaks. Three points were repeatedly made by bungalow residents about their motivations for moving to Hartrigg Oaks:

- that Hartrigg Oaks offered sufficiently comprehensive services to ensure a further move would not be necessary, because of the on-site care home

- that anxieties associated with experiencing a deterioration in health were removed, from concerns about a deterioration in quality of life through to worries that children and grandchildren would be pressured into becoming carers

- among older people living as couples, that should one partner become seriously ill, the on-site care home could allow them to both remain residents at Hartrigg Oaks.

> The thought that when you became ill you didn't have to be moved off. That was the most important feature as far as I was concerned

> We had researched it, the literature we went into very closely, the finance we went into closely, because it was going to be very expensive, but I think the thing that decided us was the fact that there's a nursing home, and I think if it weren't for that we wouldn't have bothered … because it sets your mind at rest and it can set your family's mind at rest.

> We liked the thought of having continuing care, that we could stay in our bungalow for quite a long time, and they will give us sufficient care – at least we hope they will – then we will move to The Oaks where we know people. We wouldn't be shipped off to a nursing home we didn't know, we would have friends, or if one of us had to go in a nursing home, the other could stay here [the bungalow] and visit.

Bungalow residents also reported that Hartrigg Oaks was attractive because it allowed them to decide how any future care needs they might have would be met.

> I thought well if I'm going to do anything I'd better do it while I can still be in control of it. I don't want my children to have to shove me off to somewhere.

> I thought I would never find anywhere else that would give me this degree of independence, plus communal services, plus eventual caring until you die, which is what I wanted. I think the last is very appealing because it is when you are very old and very frail that you become most of a burden to the younger members of your family, who have to choose for you. And if you've lived an independent life you want to make your own choices as much as possible.

This aspect of the decision to move by some bungalow residents showed another sort of anticipation within their preparatory moves to Hartrigg Oaks. This was a concern to retain as much control over their lives as possible, making the decisions about how their future care needs would be met while they were still fully independent. This removed responsibility and pressure from relatives, but, importantly, it also removed the capacity of relatives, or care professionals, to take over the management of care and support needs. For some residents, their preparatory moves to Hartrigg Oaks were made, at least in part, to ensure they did not lose control over their lives should they become frail.

Hartrigg Oaks was therefore seen as an attractive insurance against two risks to independence, those represented by a decline in health and those represented by having one's life taken over by others as a result of a decline in health.

The reputation of the Joseph Rowntree Foundation

That Hartrigg Oaks was operated by the JRHT had clearly been influential in attracting people to Hartrigg Oaks. Residents trusted the Rowntree name and reputation. The JRHT is an organisation with Quaker links and is therefore seen to be ethical. The JRHT is seen to have considerable financial resources and experience of running care homes and housing schemes which are highly regarded. Many residents would not have considered moving to Hartrigg Oaks if it had been established by a private-sector organisation, or a voluntary-sector organisation with a lesser reputation.

Some residents knew the JRF name because they had worked in senior management positions in social services, health care, regeneration projects or social housing. For the one-quarter of Hartrigg Oaks residents who were Quakers, JRF was known through its strong Quaker links. In the 2000 survey, 70 per cent of those residents who were members of the Society of Friends reported that JRF's strong links to the Quakers had been a reason for moving to Hartrigg Oaks.

Fee structure

Half of the bungalow residents who responded to the 2000 survey reported that they had been attracted to Hartrigg Oaks by the fee package it offered. The standard Community Fee, which guaranteed that the costs did not increase in relation to residents' use of care services, was a great incentive.

Bungalow residents who had investigated options other than Hartrigg Oaks generally compared the fees favourably with the costs of receiving equivalent support in other settings. Many pointed out that had they remained in their existing homes and sought intensive domiciliary support or eventually residential care, the costs would have been much higher. Private-sector provision, both care and insurance against the cost of future care, were generally seen as extortionately expensive by those who had investigated it.

> My wife had her mother in a nursing home and we had seen the 'evil', as I put it, of having to pay the capital to stay in a state nursing home, and I'd looked at insuring ourselves, so the financial amounts to come in here weren't so drastic when one realises what it does cost for that type of insurance …

> We didn't want to squander the kids' inheritance, but if one of us had had to go into a nursing home it would have cost £17,000 per year at that time, and that was two or three years ago, and if both of us had to go, one shudders to think.

The flexibility of payment arrangements also attracted some residents to Hartrigg Oaks. Some younger residents had moved to Hartrigg Oaks on 'fee for care', with the option that they could move to a standard or reduced Community Fee when they reached 70.

A community of like-minded people

> When we came we knew that there would be nice professional people here because of the cost, and that has happened and people are very nice here.

Survey responses indicated that just under half of the bungalow residents had been attracted to Hartrigg Oaks by the presence of like-minded people but, during interview, few residents suggested that the relative exclusivity of the scheme was attractive, indeed several residents reported feeling uncomfortable that Hartrigg Oaks was only open to them as an option because of their financial position. However, the costs of residence at Living at Hartrigg Oaks had nevertheless led some to assume that the majority of their fellow residents would be retired professional people with whom they would have shared characteristics, and this had been an attraction for some bungalow residents.

Location

> ... it's such a very good cultural centre, I came from the depths of [rural county] and to avail myself of concerts and lectures was really quite a task, but it's so accessible here, and it's just enabled me to explore all sorts of different things.

The location of Hartrigg Oaks had attracted residents to the scheme for three main reasons:

- location within York, an attractive city with many facilities and good communications

- the position of the Hartrigg Oaks site close to the city centre and the neighbouring village of Haxby, adjacent to York's outer ring road

- the attractiveness of the site more generally, within the garden village of New Earswick, which is largely made up of well-maintained turn of the century redbrick terraced homes with gardens and green areas, with adjoining fields on one side of the Hartrigg Oaks site.

Site layout, design and amenities

> We were so impressed by the service, the size of the place, the way it was laid out, what it stands for, all of that was what it should be. We decided that as long as we could afford it we would do whatever possible to secure a place here.

Bungalow residents who had toured the site prior to making a decision to move to Hartrigg Oaks had often been impressed by the range of facilities on offer. The restaurant, coffee shop, arts and crafts room and other services and amenities on site were all reported as having been influential in decisions to move to Hartrigg Oaks.

Social activities

> Once I saw the notice board and the things that were going on that people were organising for themselves, this seemed the place to be at.

The possibility of becoming isolated in the future (for example through bad health, rural location of their former homes, the future necessity of giving up driving) was an important factor in bungalow residents' decisions to leave their former homes. The interviews conducted with residents in 2000 and 2002 showed how important the potential for companionship was to some residents in deciding to move to Hartrigg Oaks.

> The main reason was the inevitability of losing one's partner, to make friends and companions before one of us – as would inevitably be the case – departed this life.

As noted above, women in their sixties and seventies who were living alone were the most likely to be attracted by the social activities on offer at Hartrigg Oaks.

Proximity to friends and family

Existing social support networks were an important factor in the decision to move to Hartrigg Oaks. As already noted, many bungalow residents had come from either York or North Yorkshire (71 per cent). For many residents, while the bungalow design, innovative financial arrangements and continuity of care were attractive, the decision to move to Hartrigg Oaks was in the end down to its proximity to friends and family. That said, a small number of residents reported having moved some distance specifically because of what Hartrigg Oaks had to offer.

Disincentives to moving to Hartrigg Oaks

The research design did not allow for contacting those older people who had made enquiries about Hartrigg Oaks and then decided not to live there. However, the bungalow residents were asked whether any aspects of Hartrigg Oaks had made them hesitate about moving there.

Cost of residence was the main potential disincentive and had made some bungalow residents hesitate before making the final commitment to live at Hartrigg Oaks. Bungalow residents had quite often examined the costs very carefully before they committed themselves to Hartrigg Oaks. Several had used accountants or other financial advisers to check over the arrangements and ascertain their affordability.

I came as a bit of a doubting Thomas, I backed out on the first bungalow because I got my paper and pencil out, to be quite honest, and I thought oh, all those thousands, I could go on a few cruises or something with that, but something kept bringing me back … and thank goodness it did …

Some residents, particularly younger residents, had also been concerned about moving to a community of older people. For some, it had not been an easy decision to make.

I thought long and hard and everyone told me I was stupid, because obviously I am a lot younger than everybody else here, and I was awake many nights thinking am I doing the right thing. But now I am here I have no regrets …

I know several people who would have liked to have said 'well, I don't need to come now but I would in ten years time, can I book a place?'

Moving into The Oaks

In the medium to long term, The Oaks care home will function as a resource for bungalow residents but, when Hartrigg Oaks first became operational, the JRHT took a decision to fill many of the places with people who moved directly into full-time care. This was to ensure the care home was fully operational as the community began to take in its residents.

The residents who moved into The Oaks were members of two groups. The first group were former residents of The Garth, a registered care home run by JRHT that had been located in New Earswick and which was closing down. This group of older people were mainly former residents of New Earswick and tended to be funded by social services. The second group were people who met the costs of residency in The Oaks through their own financial resources. As they were moving into The Oaks on the same basis on which they would move into any registered care home, this first group of residents were not part of the insurance-based CCRC financial model. Eventually, most of the residents of The Oaks will be former bungalow residents at Hartrigg Oaks, funded through its Community Fee or 'fee for care' arrangements.

Among former Garth residents, there were some regrets at having left a familiar environment for a new, much larger setting. The Garth had been a small residential home, converted from a farm house. Most reported that they settled into Hartrigg Oaks and expressed high levels of satisfaction as their rooms, facilities and amenities were superior. However, a few missed the more intimate setting of their former home.

We don't feel sort of at home here. It's a bigger place. A lot more people here, you know. It doesn't seem the same as when we were in the Garth. We were more homely and more homely with the carers as well. I mean they used to come and chat to us, you know, make it more homely …

The second group of residents had selected The Oaks as the registered care home where they would prefer to live. The factors influencing this group included JRHT's record in providing good-quality residential care, the quality of accommodation on offer, and the range of amenities and social activities on offer within Hartrigg Oaks.

3 Life at Hartrigg Oaks

The research aimed to develop an understanding of what aspects of life in a CCRC were the most fulfilling or challenging for residents, what facilities were most appreciated and valued by residents, and to explore the reasons why some people might find it more difficult to settle and establish social networks. This chapter is structured around the following broad headings:

- overall satisfaction

- living in a community of older people

- activities and social networks

- ageing at Hartrigg Oaks

- resident participation

- design, amenities and location

- affordability

- Hartrigg Oaks and the wider community

- factors influencing overall satisfaction.

Overall satisfaction

As shown in Figure 3, half the bungalow residents described themselves as 'very satisfied' with Hartrigg Oaks in both the 2000 and 2002 surveys. Just over one-third of residents described themselves as being 'quite satisfied' in 2000, with just under one-third reporting being 'quite satisfied' in 2002. Only a small number reported that they were 'neither satisfied nor dissatisfied' (shown as 'neutral'), while very small numbers reported overall dissatisfaction with Hartrigg Oaks (less than 1 per cent in 2000 and less than 5 per cent in 2002).

Similar levels of satisfaction were reported by residents of The Oaks; just over half the residents who responded to the 2000 and 2002 surveys reported they were 'very satisfied', with almost all the others reporting they were 'quite satisfied'. Across all the residents of Hartrigg Oaks there were no significant differences in levels of satisfaction between different age groups or between men and women.

> I think it's a fantastic place to live, I mean you've got security, company and lots of things going on, I mean if I had to stay where I was, I was terribly dependent on either a bike or a car, because I don't walk that well, it was getting worse and worse, I was getting that I didn't bother to go out in the evenings because it was dark, whereas here it's super.

Figure 3 Overall satisfaction with Hartrigg Oaks (by percentage of bungalow residents)

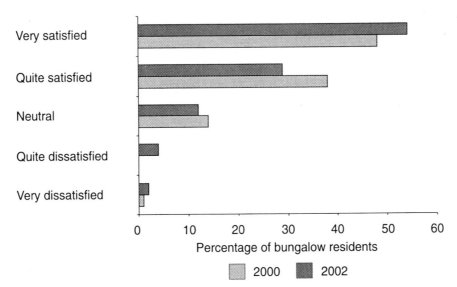

Percentage of bungalow residents

2000   2002

Source: 2000 and 2002 postal surveys. Base: 177 (2000); 152 (2002) residents

I must say that after nearly four years I cannot find a thing to grumble at …

As shown in Figure 4, bungalow residents almost all reported that Hartrigg Oaks offered them independence, privacy and a sense that help was close by. They also frequently reported that the company offered by fellow residents, the amenities, feeling safe from crime (shown as 'safe') and good care staff were good points about life at Hartrigg Oaks. Four-fifths of bungalow residents also reported that there being no pressure to take part in arranged activities (shown as 'no forced activities') was a good point about life at Hartrigg Oaks. A majority of residents also reported that residents' having a say in how Hartrigg Oaks was run was a good point about living there.

A majority also reported that the presence of 'like-minded people' was a positive aspect of life at Hartrigg Oaks and that people with differing levels of care and support need mixed together well within the community (shown as 'differing needs mix'). Two-thirds reported that Hartrigg Oaks could meet the needs of frail older people (shown as 'meets frail needs').

The findings of the 2000 survey were nearly identical to the findings of the 2002 survey. Residents of The Oaks who responded to the 2000 and 2002 survey also gave very similar answers to these questions.

Living in a community of older people

Concepts of community

The research clearly showed that residents and staff felt a 'community' was developing at Hartrigg Oaks. However, residents understood the concept of 'community' in a variety of ways. For most, the concept centred on general good neighbourliness, which was strengthened and added to by the opportunities for social interaction through the various resident-led groups and amenities such as the coffee shop. In discussion and interview, some people reported that they had come to Hartrigg Oaks determined to contribute and be active members of the emerging community. Others, however, had found the idea of being part of a community quite challenging, or simply preferred not to mix very much as they were not 'social animals' or because they already had existing social and family networks.

> What surprised us a little bit was how under used the communal facilities are and we wondered therefore was it the case that only some people here had a sense of wanting to be in a community and that most people just felt they wanted to be looked after in their old age and have a nice little bungalow. And that still puzzles me a little ... as to what extent people are committed to the sense of living in a community ...

> We all live in the same place, are subject to the same financial obligations and occupancy regulations, and that is all that binds us together. Some people want to have a 'community' and others don't. It's just an ordinary place.

> We haven't joined things here, we don't need to yet, because we are still active outside. We regard ourselves as living here, but as socially involved outside ... and we did wonder if people would be resentful, but we've never felt anything ...

The extent to which individuals participated in the emerging community was seen to be entirely their own choice, and this lack of pressure to participate was greatly valued by most residents. Many residents had been attracted to Hartrigg Oaks, in large part, by the self-contained and independent life it could offer (see Figure 4).

> It did indicate it was a community, but you didn't have to be a very active participant if you didn't want to, and that was clear and that was important – that facilities were available if you wanted them, but there weren't any red coats coming round.

Figure 4 Good points about living at Hartrigg Oaks (by percentage of bungalow residents)

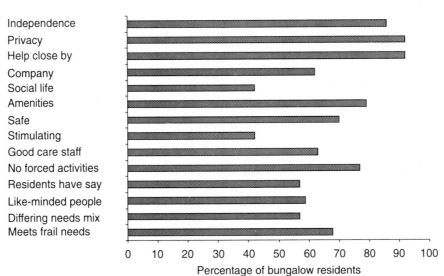

Percentage of bungalow residents

Source: 2000 and 2002 postal surveys. Base: 177 (2000); 152 (2002) residents

Settling in at Hartrigg Oaks

The majority of residents had moved into their bungalows within the first few months of Hartrigg Oaks' becoming operational. Services on site were still developing, and social networks were yet to evolve, but everyone was 'new together'. Many of the residents who were the first to arrive spoke of feeling like 'pioneers'.

The experience of new arrivals during 2001–02 was quite different. Only 24 new residents arrived during this period, as bungalows became vacant through existing residents moving to The Oaks, dying or, in a handful of cases, leaving the community. Their expectations reflected having visited Hartrigg Oaks as a working CCRC, whereas some of the first residents had made their decision to move to Hartrigg Oaks based on presentations of what would be on offer, viewing plans and visiting the site before it was fully completed.

Moving house is recognised to be a stressful experience for anyone at any stage of life; however, many of the 'pioneer' residents felt that moving to Hartrigg Oaks had been quite traumatic. The importance of 'preparatory moves' in anticipation of illness and frailty was discussed in the last chapter, and there was sometimes a feeling that this was a 'final' move.

> To come here you have to admit that you're older, which is very hard to admit. And that the future might hold more disabilities for you. You have to be realistic. So I think you have to look ahead, OK I'm in that age group. Actually I'm above

average age. You know that I'm going to be – before too many years have gone – I'm going to be facing death myself, or a lot of my friends. And I think for some people it's been quite hard to see people with disabilities around here. That's something you have to be prepared for before you come.

Many of these 'pioneer' residents who were interviewed felt that they had needed more support, both practical and emotional, when they first moved in. When care staff were interviewed in 2001, they were found to have shared this view, reflecting that, in the early days of the scheme, when large groups of residents arrived more or less at the same time, there had not always been the resources to provide counselling or emotional support to newly arrived residents. One resident commented:

You sell your house, put your things into store – I played merry hell to get the bungalow finished so I could move in – you get unpacked, sort out the garden, and then you find you're living in a community. You're not used to living in a community. How closely do you get involved in that community? All that has to be learnt. I don't think anybody realised just what an upheaval of this kind meant to elderly people. I'm 82, and it's a terrific strain, and it does affect you. I wasn't ill before but I've got high blood pressure since. And I think all that has to be taken into account.

The 'pioneer' residents were also moving into a community that was not only newly operational, but which was also the first experiment with the CCRC model in the UK. Consequently, they found themselves arriving in a somewhat unsettled environment in which newly operational services were still finding their feet. As a member of Hartrigg Oaks staff interviewed in 2001 said:

The thing is, it's a new thing, and it's changing, every year from it being opened, it's changed. So it's all there for the learning, for making mistakes, for making things right, for putting things right, for making things better.

Residents who had arrived during 2000–02 did not speak about any 'trauma' associated with moving to Hartrigg Oaks in the same way. This reflected the fact that new residents were generally arriving one household at a time into an increasingly settled environment. Hartrigg Oaks was running smoothly; early 'glitches' in some service provision had been corrected. Newer arrivals also reported that their new neighbours were very welcoming, and able to offer advice and guidance. Members of the Residents' Committee welcomed new residents, and informal meetings were run to give new residents the opportunity to meet managers and staff. Newer arrivals tended to be younger than the majority of 'pioneer' residents had been when they moved in.

> We moved in and people knocked on the door and said 'I'm so and so, I live down there, if you want anything give me a ring.' We had a card from our neighbours which said unfortunately we are away but we do welcome you and look forward to meeting you when you come back. It's that sort of thing that made us feel very much at home.
> (Resident interviewed in 2002)

Some of the newer residents remarked that they had sometimes found it awkward to fit into the social networks already established by the 'pioneer' residents. Pioneer residents also recognised that it had been perhaps easier for them to make friends as 'we were all new together'. Conversely, there were some concerns among the 'pioneer' residents that the newer arrivals, who were often of early retirement age, were more likely to have existing social networks outside Hartrigg Oaks, and be less concerned with helping to sustain and develop resident-led social activities on site.

> I think it's a different type of person who's coming … I also think that those people are not looking for perhaps the community that we were when we first came, particularly when they've come from York because they've already got all their social contacts and their social commitments outside, so I doubt whether you would see them at a concert or something like that.

Activities and social networks

Social support, received through both informal and formal social interaction, is generally seen as promoting health and well-being. One of the potential advantages for older people in a retirement community is the social interaction it can provide. Social support is usually discussed in terms of either the 'buffer' theory, in which social supports are held to have a positive effect when individuals are confronted with illness and stress, or the 'main effect' model, in which social supports are held to have a constant, beneficial effect on health and well-being. Allowing for other important influences on health status (such as income), a range of social resources, including good-quality and supportive family relationships, friendships and sexual relationships, are thought to act against stress and, in turn, both reduce the likelihood of the onset of health problems and aid recovery if health problems develop (Callaghan and Morrissey, 1993; Cohen and Wills, 1985).

Various formal and informal social support networks had developed at Hartrigg Oaks. A number of quasi-formal resident-led social and interest groups were active. Some of Hartrigg's amenities, such as the meeting rooms, provided a focus for these more structured activities. Other amenities, such as the coffee shop, provided settings where people could meet more informally.

Neighbourliness

From the fieldwork, it appeared that general good neighbourliness (collecting milk or mail, keeping an eye out for neighbours' bungalows when they were away, bringing shopping, visiting when people are ill) was widespread at Hartrigg Oaks. Many residents remarked on the friendliness of their fellow residents and their willingness to help neighbours.

In 2000, some bungalow residents reported feeling somewhat overwhelmed by what they perceived as the level of need among their older neighbours. This appeared to have become less of a concern in 2002, partly it seemed because care services had become more settled and attuned to the needs of the community, but also because residents were settling into their own informal networks and support groups. The 2002 survey responses showed that 11 per cent of residents were being regularly assisted in some way by their neighbours.

By 2002, bungalow residents appeared to have established the boundaries of their 'neighbourhoods' within Hartrigg Oaks, usually their immediate neighbours on the same or adjacent closes. Many also appeared to be very clear about how much help they could reasonably offer neighbours and friends.

> We came here to be part of a community and therefore if a neighbour or friend is in need we will help, but we're not here to give continuous help … I feel under no obligation to be a good Samaritan all round the place. Different people do different things, and you can't do everything.

Some residents, although they were glad there were communal facilities and active social groups, were eager to maintain a balance between their privacy and being part of a community. Most felt it was possible to do so, although a few reported feeling that as a relatively small community, Hartrigg Oaks could be quite claustrophobic, and that there was a certain amount of gossip. Some commented it was important to them to have a 'life outside' Hartrigg Oaks.

Informal social contact

The amenities at Hartrigg Oaks, particularly the coffee shop, were seen by residents and staff to be important centres for informal social contact. Many residents commented that it had been through the coffee shop that they first got to know their fellow residents. In the 2002 postal survey, 65 per cent of bungalow residents reported that the coffee shop was 'good for socialising'.

> [in the coffee shop] … We met people, people said 'oh hello, have you just moved in and how's this and how's that', and you got all their stories about moving in and we knew an enormous amount of people in about a fortnight.

As time went on, many residents used the coffee shop as a place to reinforce existing relationships by meeting their friends there. Some reflected that this perhaps made it less of a melting pot than it had been when Hartrigg Oaks first opened. Some residents also talked about the formation of cliques and restricted social networks between some residents, which were sometimes reflected in the way in which space was used by residents within the coffee shop. This sort of pattern might be expected within any shared environment. When they were interviewed in 2001, staff reported feeling that the coffee shop offered a valuable opportunity for residents of The Oaks to meet bungalow residents and to participate in the wider life of the community. This view was shared by some of The Oaks residents interviewed in 2000 and 2002.

Resident-led activities

Residents organised their own social activities. There were various social and interest groups, all set up and organised by residents. Residents spoke about craft classes, a thriving theology group, literature groups, a concert and theatre group, a regular games night, yoga classes and the Discovering Yorkshire group which arranged regular outings.

> … all sorts of things go on here, we have a lot of music and groups of all sorts of activities, I belong to a painting group, a literary group and then there are sewing and embroidery groups and play reading, gardening, they're all on the spot … there's a theology group, very interesting lectures.
> (Resident of The Oaks)

> There are a lot of groups, we don't belong to many of them, but they are there. Certainly for people on their own it is an amazing place I'm sure, because there is no need ever for anyone to feel lonely or alone, which a lot of older people begin to feel, there's no need for that at all.

Three-quarters of the bungalow residents who responded to the 2002 survey were involved in resident-led groups or activities to some degree. Those who were involved with two or more groups/activities were more likely to report that Hartrigg Oaks was a 'stimulating place to live' (56 per cent) than those involved in one group (37 per cent) or those not regularly involved in resident-led groups or activities (19 per cent).

Many Hartrigg Oaks residents shared professional backgrounds. Some residents reflected this had facilitated the emergence of many resident-led community activities.

> Of course, we have very nice people living here, very interesting people who've done a number of things and, of course, who are extremely helpful, the younger people in their seventies, who are very helpful in doing things here, you see all these groups are run by volunteers, people on the spot …
> (Resident of The Oaks, in 2002)

While these shared backgrounds were generally regarded as an asset by the residents of Hartrigg Oaks, some residents from other backgrounds reported that they could sometimes feel out of step with the rest of the community. Despite widespread involvement in groups at Hartrigg Oaks, some residents also reported that the on-site social activities were unappealing to them. A few had a perception that Hartrigg Oaks was lacking in activities, though most thought the community offered many activities.

> We were thinking it would be more of a vibrant place, sort of mentally, to be in, because there isn't as much community activity as we expected. I mean if you go to the library here you'll hardly find anybody else there, or in this music room, there's not much going on in the music room or the restaurant. In fact the whole place is like morgue in the evening, there's hardly anything going on at all.
> (Bungalow resident, 2002)

Life outside Hartrigg Oaks

For many bungalow residents, the social support and networks that they had outside Hartrigg Oaks were as important as, or sometimes more important than, the social support they had within the community. Many talked about the importance of having a 'life outside Hartrigg Oaks' and being able to leave the community regularly on daytrips and holidays. This was strongly linked to feelings that Hartrigg Oaks was attractive because it allowed an independent life, with community participation being the individual's choice.

> … there were people who felt that this place should be self contained … I think as long as you can get out and about, do so … don't become introverted.

Residents who were from the York area already had established social networks, and often family nearby. For others new to the area, York was seen to offer many opportunities. However, some residents reported feeling that establishing social networks was more difficult for newcomers to the area.

It makes life more liveable here if you've got friends outside.

If I ever lose the use of my car I would feel dreadfully isolated.

The majority of bungalow residents responding to the 2002 survey left the Hartrigg Oaks site on a quite frequent basis. Only a minority of bungalow residents tended not to leave the site (13 per cent), while the majority left the site at least several times a month (87 per cent). One-quarter of bungalow residents reported leaving the site every day.

Seventy-seven per cent of bungalow residents went on holiday for one or more weeks a year. A high proportion were away for several weeks a year, with 56 per cent of residents reporting they were on holiday for three or more weeks a year. A small group were on holiday for several months a year.

Health status, activities and social networks

Many residents spoke warmly of the friends they had made in Hartrigg Oaks. Some reported that living in a sociable and friendly community had been an unexpected bonus of moving to Hartrigg Oaks. There were concerns, however, that some residents were isolated, especially some residents of The Oaks and those bungalow residents who were frail or disabled, or who simply found it difficult to mix.

A number of frail Hartrigg Oaks residents were taking an active part in the arranged on-site social activities. The residents of The Oaks who responded to the 2002 survey were quite likely to be involved in activities, despite an average age of 86. Almost two-thirds of Oaks respondents were involved in at least one activity (59 per cent). It must, however, be noted that only half the Oaks residents responded to the survey and that this group may well have been more representative of those who were more active.

If we can manage to fit them in, there are quite a number of things arranged by the bungalow section, there's a committee and we're invited to that and all that they do and if there are any general meetings, we're invited there ... and there's the gymnasium that's been installed and that's very good, there's a theology group, there is music, so there's quite, when we look round, there's quite a lot of activity if we're able to do it.
(Resident of The Oaks, 2002)

Some less mobile residents were also assisted when they wished to attend activities and social events. In the 2002 survey, 20 per cent of bungalow residents reported that they 'provided help with getting to social events or with meeting people' for their neighbours. In addition, residents of The Oaks reported that staff would help them if they wished to attend events or activities outside The Oaks. However, the 2002 survey also found some evidence that participation in activities was linked to age:

- Bungalow residents who participated in two or more activities had an average age of 76.

- Bungalow residents who reported that they 'rarely or never' took part in groups or activities had an average age of 83.

- Bungalow residents who participated in two or more resident-led activities were more likely to leave the Hartrigg Oaks site several times a week (81 per cent) than those who rarely or never took part in resident-led activities (52 per cent).

When combined with the interview results, these findings suggested a small population of less active, older residents who tended to be characterised by lower levels of involvement in resident-led groups and who were sometimes less likely to leave the Hartrigg Oaks site.

A number of residents of The Oaks and the bungalows were very frail and found it difficult to leave their homes. Some of these residents, when they were interviewed in 2000 and 2002, reported experiencing difficulties in joining in with the activities at Hartrigg Oaks. Varying degrees of sensory impairment were quite common, which could make social contacts quite problematic. As one visually impaired resident remarked, he could be introduced to someone, and not be able to recognise the person the next time they met. Hearing loss also limited participation for some residents in many activities. There were difficulties too for residents using wheelchairs to join in some activities such as resident-organised trips. This was because their participation required other residents to lift them, which was not always practical or possible, as the Hartrigg Oaks minibus was not wheelchair friendly. In the 2000 survey of bungalow residents, 21 per cent reported that they were involved in fewer activities than they had been before they moved to Hartrigg Oaks because of changes in their health. The figure in 2002 was slightly lower, at 15 per cent.

The views of residents on the ways in which frail or disabled residents could be involved in social activities were mixed. Some felt that it was important for residents to take a role in providing support. Others spoke about not wanting to, or feeling able to, focus their lives on providing support to other residents.

I am mindful of course of the people from The Oaks and the people who are severely physically disabled here, that there is I think a challenge there to meet their needs, to satisfy their needs. I can understand it, that some people almost confined to eat with the same two or three people for every day of their lives here who are desperate to break open … there are some real psycho-social challenges here.

… there is a willingness amongst members of the groups to help the less mobile to come and to be taken back to their bungalows or The Oaks afterwards. So I think that again is part of the growing process, you get to know people and you get to be aware of their difficulties and if you're able I think you are prepared to help …

Ageing at Hartrigg Oaks

As was shown in Chapter Two, many bungalow residents had moved to Hartrigg Oaks in anticipation that, over time, they would become less able to live independently. A number of themes related to a group of people ageing together emerged from the interviews with residents and staff, including the age range of residents, the attractiveness of a CCRC for 'young' older people, living with disability and bereavement.

Age range of residents

In January 2003, the average age of Hartrigg Oaks' residents was 78. Some residents took a highly positive view of age, emphasising their own levels of activity or drawing attention to the independence of residents in their eighties and nineties whom they knew. Some saw little distinction between Hartrigg Oaks and simply living on a street on which there was a high proportion of other retired people.

You wouldn't think you were living in an old folks' complex. It's just like anywhere else. Friends would say 'Oh, how can you live there'. Well where I lived before, I said, everyone around me was retired. They'd all gone in before me, and they'd stayed, and all their families had gone, and they're older than me most of them. So what was the difference? It's only your concept, isn't it?

A few of the bungalow residents and residents of The Oaks interviewed in 2000 and 2002 missed the presence of younger people, particularly children. However, it was clear that many preferred the sense of seclusion and security that Hartrigg Oaks offered to living in a more mixed community.

In 2000, many residents remarked on the apparent predominance of very old people in Hartrigg Oaks. A small number of residents were clearly uncomfortable, as they had expected a wider age range. By 2002, however, the focus of residents' concerns related more to maintaining a balanced age range, to keep the levels of community activity high and to ensure that Hartrigg Oaks retained what they felt was a fairly vibrant feel to it.

> I was surprised at the age of the residents, I find they're all in their seventies, eighties, nineties, it would have been nice to have more people nearer my own age.
> (Bungalow resident, 2000)

> I can see it's terribly important that we do have younger people, otherwise we shall all be decrepit.
> (Bungalow resident, 2002)

Some residents felt that a retirement community would be less attractive to people in their sixties, if there was a predominance of very old people. However, some of the younger residents reported benefits in moving to Hartrigg Oaks in early retirement, saying it was easier to settle, cope with the move, and make friends both within and outside the community.

Living with disability

Although bungalow residents were attracted by the continuing care offered by Hartrigg Oaks, a small number found it difficult to adjust to life in a community that provided extensive support and care services. In 2000, a few of the younger and more able-bodied bungalow residents had clearly found it distressing to be in an environment with disabled people. Most residents, however, felt that this was something residents of a CCRC should have expected and have been prepared for. Staff, when they were interviewed in 2001, also reflected on what they felt were sometimes negative attitudes towards disability in the community. They felt that there were tensions between bungalow residents and residents of The Oaks.

> ... but if you are not in your eighties you think, gosh, meeting folks who are very disabled, it's bringing the future in front of your eyes, and yet you are trying to remain active and very interested in things. And you think goodness, I'm going to be like that. It's very depressing. One doesn't like to talk about these things, it's getting more and more depressing.
> (Bungalow resident, 2000)

During the 2002 fieldwork, the experience of disability appeared to have become more familiar and personal; residents expressed their sadness, sometimes shock, at seeing the deterioration in the health of neighbours and friends. Some residents were 'inspired' by the resilience and determination of neighbours to overcome health problems, and others spoke with great appreciation of the support and kindness they received from staff and other residents when they had themselves become ill.

> Some people who spoke up quite loudly at the beginning about the disabled have quietened down, sometimes because they have become disabled, or just gained greater understanding about why things are as they are.
> (Bungalow resident, 2002)

Dementia was an ongoing concern. In 2000, some bungalow residents had expressed concern about neighbours who were becoming confused. Staff, when interviewed in 2001, also reflected that a few residents were not comfortable around people with dementia, and were saddened by such attitudes. In 2002, again perhaps reflecting the 'settling down' of the community, and open discussions between residents and the Trust regarding the future of dementia care, some residents remarked that it was becoming clearer to what extent the community could support residents with dementia-type illnesses. This issue is discussed in Chapter 4.

Quite a high proportion of residents of The Oaks were too unwell to participate in the fieldwork. Among those who were more active, as has already been noted, there were some individuals who participated in social activities. A few were conscious that they made a handful of the other residents uncomfortable, but this was again something that was reported more frequently in 2000 than in 2002.

> ... you can meet them [bungalow residents] month after month in the coffee shop and you don't get a smile out of them, or a hello or anything, but that is only some of them.
> (Resident of The Oaks, 2000)

> I get on well with the people here. I meet people through the restaurant, music, theology, mostly organised through the bungalow people.
> (Resident of The Oaks, 2002)

The changing nature of The Oaks, which was originally largely filled with former residents of another care home and older people who moved directly into its beds, may have partly explained the more positive attitudes reported in 2002. The Oaks was beginning to be seen as a integral part of Hartrigg Oaks by the bungalow residents, as increasing numbers of their former neighbours took up temporary or permanent residence within it (see Chapter 4).

Death and bereavement

Residents of The Oaks and the bungalows, spoke with great sorrow about friends who had died. A few residents who were interviewed in 2002 had experienced several losses within a relatively very short period and were the only surviving member of a group of friends; such losses were keenly felt. Some felt a loss not only in the sense of Hartrigg Oaks losing an individual, but also the contact with the families of those individuals. Some residents and staff reported wondering how well the community would cope over time with the death of residents and consequent accumulation of feelings of loss and bereavement.

During the 2000 fieldwork, some residents thought that there was a need for bereavement counselling. The possibility of providing such counselling had been considered by staff and, on reflection, it was felt that it would inappropriate for on-site staff to provide such counselling for residents; where necessary, staff could refer residents to specialist services such as CRUSE.

The death of residents was also, of course, a difficult issue for staff, especially those who were new to a nursing and care environment. Apart from the sense of loss for the individual, there were the very practical aspects of death – the undertaker being called, grieving relatives to be comforted – that had, before first confronted, not always been something that new non-care staff had really thought of as part of the job. Since Hartrigg Oaks opened, a number of bungalow residents had died in their own homes, and this had presented particular challenges for the Home Care staff, which were being addressed through staff training sessions.

Resident participation

Hartrigg Oaks had an elected Residents' Committee and various sub-committees. In 2000, many residents felt it was extremely important to have active resident participation, to enable residents to have their say and be consulted, and also to allow the management to gather feedback and opinion from the residents. Most residents felt that they were able to express their views through the Residents' Committee or directly to JRHT staff. A small number of residents felt that resident representation was completely inadequate, and that residents should have greater control.

During the 2002 fieldwork, the participants in focus groups and interviews took a more circumspect view of resident participation than they had in 2000. A prolonged and clearly acrimonious dispute among residents over whether there should be an additional charge for the health activity centre that was opened in 2001 had led to this change of view. Some felt that there were a small minority of residents who were negative and very vociferous, complaining about minor things with great alacrity. A few residents reported feeling inclined to disengage with the resident participation process and wondered about finding recruits to take seats on the Residents' Committee, as it was seen by some to be an onerous and relatively thankless task.

Views were mixed on the extent to which JRHT was able to take residents' views into account. A few felt well represented, and a few felt not at all well represented; most felt they were consulted by JRHT, but that it was only realistic and practical to expect that the management would ultimately take the major decisions about the running of Hartrigg Oaks.

> People come here thinking it's democratic but it's not. We're lucky we are consulted to the extent that we are, but in the end they make the decisions and we have no representation at the decision making level.
> (Bungalow resident 2002)

In talking to some of the women residents, there was a shared perception that some of the male residents struggled with retirement and the loss of status they had enjoyed in their working lives. Women sometimes felt that adapting to life in Hartrigg Oaks and accepting later life with its challenges and constraints was more difficult for some of the male residents. Women reported that some men tried to dominate whatever setting they found themselves in. This could also make some elements of resident participation, and indeed some more informal activity, difficult for some women. Other research has found similar gender issues arising in other retirement communities (Brenton, 1999).

> There just seem to be so many instances of the men not really sure what they are going to do with themselves to maintain whatever status …
> (Bungalow resident, 2002)

> I think that men find it harder to come here and accept their retirement and I think that some of them are looking for a substitute job, and it's lovely if it can be channelled into the right things …
> (Bungalow resident, 2002)

Staff attitudes to resident empowerment were mixed. When they were interviewed in late 2001, staff were generally supportive of the residents having more control. Staff also understood that Hartrigg Oaks was designed to enable greater choice and independence for its residents. However, some staff spoke about a lack of clear 'boundaries' that defined the circumstances where residents should be consulted. In particular, it was felt by staff that many residents were generally very reluctant to see changes or innovations when it meant increases in their fees, and that the process of consultation could be slow and unwieldy.

Some staff felt that residents had been allowed 'too much power' and were allowed to be too demanding. In part it was felt that this reflected the nature of the scheme where residents are paying considerable sums of money. However, some staff also felt that it partly reflected the social class and life experiences of the residents, who were often retired managers.

Design, amenities and location

Design of the bungalows

Table 1 shows the views of residents about their bungalows. Most reported that they thought their bungalows were either very well designed or quite well designed (85 per cent in 2000, 88 per cent in 2002).

When interviewed, residents praised the spaciousness of their bungalows, and many had opted to convert the loft space into an additional room. The small and manageable gardens and distinct boundaries between properties were also valued, as was the allocation of a parking space. Residents also appreciated that the Lifetime Homes standard bungalows were designed to allow wheelchair access. The alarm call system connecting every bungalow to The Oaks Centre was reported as providing a sense of security. As noted in Chapter 2, many of these features had attracted residents to Hartrigg Oaks.

Two basic elements of the design of the bathroom, the decision to fit a certain kind of toilet, which many residents found to have an inadequate flush, and particularly, a bath which many residents found too low and shallow to use, were the most criticised features of the bungalows' design. Some Hartrigg Oaks residents, when

Table 1 Views of bungalow design

Quality of design	2000 survey	2002 survey
Very well designed	42 %	40 %
Quite well designed	43 %	48 %
Neither well nor badly designed	8 %	7 %
Not very well designed	4 %	4 %
Poorly designed	2 %	1 %
Base	177	151

Percentages are rounded. Source: 2002 postal survey

they were interviewed in 2000, could not use their bath. Programmes to assist residents who could not use their baths and to replace the toilets were ongoing as the research drew to a close. When asked about the features of Hartrigg Oaks that might be improved in the 2000 survey, 44 per cent of bungalow residents reported 'better design of bathrooms'. The figure for the 2002 survey was 49 per cent.

Other design problems including the position of the meters at a low level within the bungalows, rather than outside, where they could be read without someone entering the house. There were also small locking mechanisms on the windows that were difficult for people with poor eyesight or arthritis. Smaller numbers of residents remarked on poor soundproofing, especially where the living room of one bungalow was adjacent to the bedroom of the neighbouring bungalow. Many residents are hard of hearing and need to have televisions or radios turned up loud. A small number of residents found their living rooms cold and had paid to have extra radiators installed.

Other aspects of design

Residents of The Oaks generally praised the size of their rooms and were also pleased to have en suite facilities. However, a few felt that some of the rooms did not have a very interesting view, which is more of a consideration when one is less mobile. In addition, a few reported feeling that the appearance of the interior of The Oaks was seen by some as lacking character or as having a different, more institutional, feel than the rest of Hartrigg Oaks.

> It has to be more like a hotel I think, because that was the impression we got, when we first came in, walking along corridors, going round, finding our way ... (Resident of The Oaks, 2002)

The design, facilities and amenities of the Oaks Centre were generally praised. The purposely uneven paving slabs in the main foyer (supposed to give the space the feel of a thoroughfare) were roundly criticised, as they were felt to be hazardous to residents using wheelchairs or zimmer frames. Some residents felt the coffee shop was too small and its design had not taken account of the number of people who would access this area in wheelchairs or electric buggies. A few residents thought that more 'tactile' (i.e. 3D models or braille) signing and mapping would be helpful to residents with visual impairment who might find themselves disorientated or lost.

Some bungalow residents felt that bungalows were tightly clustered together on the site, meaning that they were closer to some of the neighbours than they ideally would have liked. Many residents had enjoyed seeing the planting and gardens mature, and appreciated the careful maintenance of the grounds. Some residents felt there should be more benches, or small enclosed formal garden areas where people could sit and meet other residents. Dropped curbs and level pavements were appreciated by wheelchair uses and others with mobility or sight problems, and moving about the site was generally thought to be safe and easy.

Amenities

The range of amenities and facilities at Hartrigg Oaks was widely praised and seen to be key to promoting the development of social networks. For some residents who were not able to leave the site very easily, the opportunity to 'eat out' on-site or to take part in on-site activities were greatly valued.

Figure 5 shows that the most popular amenities among bungalow residents included the restaurant and coffee shop (shown as 'Catering'), the music room (i.e. events staged within this meeting room), the health activity centre (shown as 'Gym') and the hairdressing service.

Just under one-third of the bungalow residents reported that they often used the shop, a similar proportion used the library, while one-quarter reported that they often used the arts and crafts facilities. Just under one-quarter went on resident-arranged people-carrier trips, which included both shopping runs and daytrips (many residents retained the use of a car). Almost all The Oaks residents who responded to the survey reported that they used the coffee shop and restaurant in particular, but also the library, arts and crafts rooms, hairdresser and health activity centre.

Figure 5 Percentage of bungalow residents 'often' using Hartrigg Oaks amenities

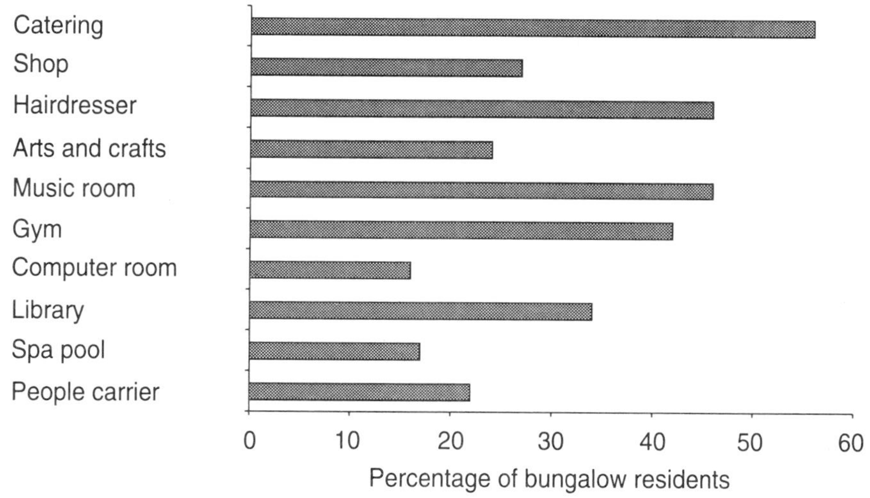

Source: 2002 postal survey. Base: 152 residents

The 2000 and 2002 interviews showed that the coffee shop was seen by residents and staff to be the main social hub of Hartrigg Oaks. The more formal restaurant, adjacent to the coffee shop, was felt to offer frailer residents a good venue for celebrating special occasions and as a means of entertaining visitors.

Comments on the standard of catering at Hartrigg Oaks were generally favourable, although there was a range of views. Most residents thought the catering staff were kind and helpful, and some remarked on the rudeness of some residents towards the catering staff, and their readiness to complain. Most of the catering staff were young people, and it was felt by staff that some residents' attitudes could be patronising towards them. There had been training sessions for the young staff about working with older people, and these were generally regarded as successful.

> The disadvantage is that there is familiarity because the same people are in, you don't just get an awkward customer once and never again, and you get them everyday, and likewise for them [the residents], if they don't get on with whoever is serving on in the coffee shop, they are stuck with them as well. (Member of staff, 2001)

Table 2 shows that those residents who were making the most use of Hartrigg Oaks amenities also tended to be those people who were most involved in resident-led groups and activities. These findings suggest that those Hartrigg Oaks residents who were characterised by tending not to participate in resident-led groups and activities (who were also less likely to leave the site regularly) also made less use of the amenities at Hartrigg Oaks.

Location

York and North Yorkshire were considered attractive places to live by the majority of residents. Hartrigg Oaks was also quite close to York district hospital, the GP practice for the area and other health services. Public transport links provided access to local shops and the city centre.

Table 2 Use of amenities by bungalow residents by participation in resident-led activities

No. of groups and resident-led activities in which involved	Did not often use any amenities (%)	Often used 1–2 amenities (%)	Often used 3–4 amenities (%)	Often used 5 or more amenities (%)
Two or more groups or activities	–	31	48	21
One group or activity	8	41	42	6
No groups or activities	29	49	22	–

Percentages are rounded. Source: 2002 postal survey

Quite a number of bungalow residents had cars; the older residents were concerned about reapplying for driving licences and their ability to continue to drive, as they felt to be without a car would seriously affect their quality of life. It was recognised that those residents who are not able to leave the site easily, usually the frailer and older residents, were more limited in what they could do and in the facilities they could access, as poor mobility or sensory impairment could undermine someone's ability to use public transport.

Many residents and staff felt that many less mobile people, particularly Oaks residents, would appreciate more regular outings and trips, and needed better access to shops, banks and other services. There had been plans to have a cash point machine on site, however, it had not proved possible. Consequently, some residents were allowed to cash cheques in the coffee shop as part of their care plan.

Affordability

A few bungalow residents had hesitated before finally committing to Hartrigg Oaks because of the costs involved, others had been attracted by a financial package[1] that would be advantageous to them should they develop significant ongoing care needs. Figure 6 shows the views of bungalow residents on the affordability of Hartrigg Oaks.

Figure 6 How easy is it to afford Hartrigg Oaks? (by percentage of bungalow residents)

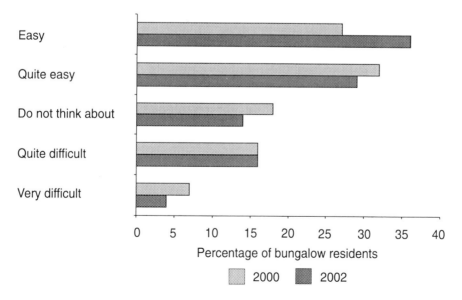

Source: 2000 and 2002 postal surveys. Base: 177 (2000) and 152 (2002) residents

Between 2000 and 2002, there had been a number of economic changes, most notably a fall in interest rates and reductions on the stock market, that may have adversely affected the incomes of some Hartrigg Oaks residents. As shown in Figure 6, however, there were few changes in the reported affordability of Hartrigg Oaks between 2000 and 2002. In both years, the majority of bungalow residents reported that Hartrigg Oaks was 'easy' or 'quite easy' to afford (59 per cent in 2000 and 65 per cent in 2002). Some residents also reported that they 'did not think about' affordability.

Nevertheless, one-fifth of residents reported some difficulty in affording Hartrigg Oaks in 2002. The 2002 survey also found that one-third of bungalow residents reported that Hartrigg Oaks had become more difficult for them to afford since they moved in. Although half this group still reported Hartrigg was affordable or quite affordable, half reported it was quite difficult or very difficult to afford. Looking at these data another way, it could be seen that almost all of those people who reported Hartrigg Oaks was quite or very difficult to afford also reported that it had become more difficult to afford since they moved in (86 per cent).

> Certainly if some people's income was dependent on investment income, then it would be a lot more difficult for some people now to consider this, as indeed some residents are a lot more concerned than they perhaps were 18 months ago.

Some residents reported that, compared with the costs of living in their former home, Hartrigg Oaks had not worked out to be as expensive as they had expected.

> … it's not quite as expensive as I thought it would be, there are perks, outside decoration, central heating servicing, immediate repairs when the kitchen fan falls out. I was totting up one day what I was paying living alone in a bungalow and there's a considerable saving, plus the mental comfort of having things seen to, and the insurance, we only have to insure our contents.

In 2002, some bungalow residents were clearly worried about whether they would be able to continue to afford to live at Hartrigg Oaks given continuing falls in interest rates and stock markets. Some married women expressed concern about their future financial status should their partner die before them, and the main pension be lost. JRHT have established a separate new charity, The Hartrigg Oaks Charitable Trust, which is partly funded by annual transfers from residents' Community Fees, specifically to assist residents who find themselves in financial difficulties, and many residents spoke about this and the reassurance it gave.

You may pick up by talking to some people here, they're very worried, I think the women are very worried, that if they lose their husbands, their pension is going to come crashing down, depends on the generosity of the pension schemes and I think a lot of people, while they know that hopefully, they know they can cope, another thing that is important, is the charitable trust they've brought forward, so certain people who've come could be beginning to worry, 'if I live another 15 years', it's a concern and I think that they are reassured …

The relative cost of care at Hartrigg Oaks was praised by some residents. They drew attention to the much higher levels of expenditure that would have been involved in using means-tested community care and the high cost of private-sector care.

Some residents expressed concerns that access to Hartrigg Oaks was largely restricted to an affluent minority. This was supported by JRHT, which has estimated that one-quarter of older people in the UK can afford a CCRC with equivalent costs to Hartrigg. Many recognised that they were in a relatively privileged situation compared with many older people. This group felt that ways of extending access to CCRCs should be investigated.

This is my doubt about Hartrigg Oaks – I love it here, it's very pleasant, I am very fortunate to be so active, and I can afford it because I have savings and a good pension – but for a number of people it would be too expensive …

I think it's a marvellous scheme, I would like to see it extended all over the country, not just for people who can afford to buy, but for all older people for their safety, security and care.

In 2000, many residents who had chosen the refundable Residence Fee remarked that the sum refunded to their estate when they died would relate to the market price of the bungalow at the time when they entered Hartrigg Oaks, and would not reflect any increase in property prices over time. There were some concerns about the fairness of this arrangement, and the potential 'profit' the JRHT would make on re-selling the bungalows. Property prices rose by more than one-quarter in York between 2000 and 2002. By 2002, more residents remarked on the 'profits' that JRHT had made re-selling bungalows. This issue had been recognised and was being discussed by the JRHT, given the extent of house price inflation in areas of the UK over 2001–02. It was noted by JRHT, however, that the 'profits' from bungalow sales were returned to Hartrigg Oaks own ring-fenced budget, with no sum being retained by the JRHT.

For a very small number of residents, the refundable Residence Fee arrangement was seen as effectively preventing them from leaving Hartrigg Oaks, as the sum they would receive if they chose to leave would no longer be sufficient to allow them to re-enter the housing market. There seemed to be no obvious 'exit strategy' once their financial resources were tied into the community.

Hartrigg Oaks and the wider community

Hartrigg Oaks was built on a greenfield site at the edge of the garden village of New Earswick,[2] which is mainly made up of social housing managed by JRHT. Hartrigg Oaks was originally intended to become part of the wider community of New Earswick.

Over time, small numbers of Hartrigg Oaks residents had become more involved with various activities in the village, attending various churches, the Friends Meeting House, Parish Council meetings, and other groups. Hartrigg Oaks had also provided employment opportunities for many villagers. Beyond this, however, there was little evidence of much interaction between the two communities during 2000–02. In the 2000 survey, 48 per cent of respondents thought Hartrigg Oaks was 'separate' from New Earswick, with a slightly higher level being found in 2002 (56 per cent). Residents at Hartrigg Oaks felt they were seen by villagers to be affluent and privileged, enjoying facilities that were not available to village residents.

A small group of New Earswick residents who were interviewed in 2002 felt that a retirement community was more welcome than other possible developments (for example, executive homes); they noted that the older (and sometimes frail) residents of Hartrigg Oaks could not be expected to take an active part in village life. They also felt that the facilities at Hartrigg Oaks would probably not be of great interest to the majority of village residents. It was also pointed out by New Earswick residents that community participation within the existing village was not particularly extensive, and it was perhaps unrealistic to expect Hartrigg Oaks residents to participate more actively in village life than villagers themselves.

It had been suggested that New Earswick residents could use the restaurant or coffee shop, or join some of the activity groups, as a way of developing relationships between the two communities. Some Hartrigg Oaks residents were, however, unwilling to share facilities for which they were paying considerable sums of money. Reports of teenage and child nuisance within the village concerned a few of the residents of Hartrigg Oaks. Community safety and anti-social behaviour were also recognised as obstacles to greater integration by New Earswick residents, when they were interviewed in 2002.

There's a lot of poor people in the village, you know, and they have a lot of difficulty with their children, in a way, parts of the village are like council housing estates, because they are poor, they're paying rent, they don't have pride in their property, naturally they resent us taking their field away, so it's natural they resent us ... gradually as the village, every third house that comes on apparently, is sold, so the number of owner occupiers will increase and it does sound very elitist, but I am sure that's what the division is, I think it is a kind of income, status division ...
(Hartrigg Oaks resident, 2002)

... we as a village community, excluding Hartrigg Oaks, have been concerned for many years about levels of security in the village, problem of youth nuisance, vandalism, drug abuse, alcohol abuse, largely by young people, which we have made very considerable efforts to counteract ... we're aware that it isn't anything like as bad in this village as it is in other parts of York, we are concerned that it doesn't deteriorate, we're concerned that we should try and improve it. Now, by definition those concerns are even more strongly felt in an elderly retirement community and Hartrigg Oaks by its geographical isolation, and by the way it has been planned and set up, is very largely free of that difficulty at the moment, and I'm quite sure that Hartrigg Oaks residents feel that it should stay that way ...
(New Earswick resident, 2002)

Factors influencing overall satisfaction

Statistical analysis indicated that several factors had a bearing on the level of overall satisfaction with Hartrigg Oaks reported by bungalow residents. Some of the findings were perhaps surprising, as it was found that views on the affordability of Hartrigg Oaks were not significantly linked to how satisfied bungalow residents were with life at Hartrigg Oaks.

Figure 7 shows some of the differences between the views of bungalow residents who were 'very satisfied' with Hartrigg Oaks and those who were 'quite satisfied'. Those who reported being 'very satisfied' were more likely to report that Hartrigg had a 'good social life' (62 per cent), was a 'stimulating place to live' (64 per cent) and offered 'company so it was not lonely' (81 per cent). In contrast, those who were 'quite satisfied' were much less likely to report that Hartrigg Oaks offered a good social life (31 per cent), was a stimulating place to live (26 per cent) or offered company (48 per cent).

Figure 7 Comparison of views between 'very satisfied' and 'quite satisfied' bungalow residents

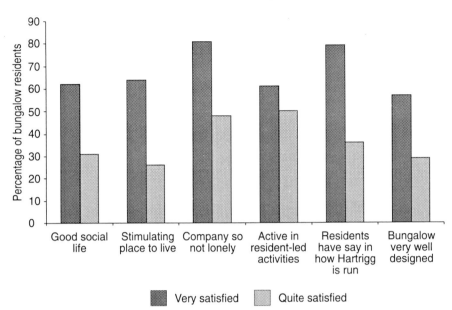

Source: 2002 postal survey. Base: 120 residents

Bungalow residents who reported that they were quite satisfied overall were also much less likely to share the view that 'residents have a say in how Hartrigg Oaks is run' (36 per cent compared with 79% among very satisfied residents). They were also less likely to view their bungalow as 'very well designed' than 'very satisfied' bungalow residents.

These findings suggested that the extent to which Hartrigg Oaks acted as a social resource for its residents influenced overall satisfaction. There were also indications that views on resident participation and bungalow design had an influence on overall satisfaction.

It is important to view these findings in the context of very small numbers of bungalow residents expressing actual dissatisfaction with Hartrigg Oaks. It must also be noted that only low numbers of residents reported that they were 'neither satisfied nor dissatisfied' with Hartrigg Oaks (see Figure 3).

4 Care and support

This chapter examines resident views on the support and care services at Hartrigg Oaks. It reviews bungalow residents' views of the services delivered to their bungalows and then examines residents' views of The Oaks. The chapter concludes with a discussion of the management of dementia within Hartrigg Oaks.

Support and care services at Hartrigg Oaks

During the period of the research, the support and care services[1] provided at Hartrigg Oaks included:

- the 'Handyman' service, which undertook small repairs and maintenance for bungalow residents who required it

- the 'Home Help' service, which offers vacuuming, dusting, washing up, changing beds, mattress turning, laundering of clothing, bed linen and towels and a basic shopping service for food and cleaning materials (providing a service to an average of one-third of bungalows during 2002)

- the 'Pop-in' service, providing up to 15 minutes of emotional support, meal delivery and some lower levels of personal care such as toileting or meal preparation to bungalow residents, a more intensive service than its name suggested (typically supporting 25–27 bungalow residents during 2002)

- the 'Personal Care' service, providing assistance with dressing, undressing, bathing, toileting, meal preparation, assistance with medication to bungalow residents (typically supporting 15–18 bungalow residents during 2002)

- short and interim stays within The Oaks for bungalow residents (during 2002, 674 bed-nights were provided to 23 residents, averaging a stay of 29 nights each)

- permanent residence within The Oaks registered care home, which involved a resident 'selling' their bungalow (if they live alone).

Assessment and service planning

Support and care services at Hartrigg Oaks were accessed through an assessment process carried out by the care professionals among the staff. Residents could not simply request any services they wanted. The decision as to how their needs were best met ultimately rested with the care professionals at Hartrigg Oaks.

By 2002, the assessment process was viewed positively by the great majority of residents and staff. The organisation of care and support was also generally seen as being effective.

During 2000, views on care assessment had been rather more mixed. Some bungalow residents had arrived with an expectation that support and care would be provided when they wanted it.

> We had the impression if we needed it, or thought we needed it, we would get it, whereas it was quite recently we've heard the real emphasis that care is provided in the light of a care assessment and not just because we want it. (Bungalow resident, 2000)

The extent to which this expectation of support on request was due to residents' interpretations of sales information on Hartrigg Oaks, or whether that information was in any sense ambiguous, was not a question the research analysed. It may also be that some people were unfamiliar with the concept of 'assessment', having had little or no contact with welfare services.

In 2000, some bungalow residents expressed concerns about whether they would have access to the services they needed. There was a worry that The Oaks might not have sufficient space, because it had filled some of its beds with direct placements when it first opened. There was also a feeling there had been an underestimate of the need for low-level domestic help (the 'Home Help' service). Concerns were also voiced that in order to ensure that its bungalows were all occupied, Hartrigg Oaks had initially taken in more frail older people than the community was designed to deal with.

> The thing that did alarm us a little was to find they had practically filled The Oaks … a lot of people were annoyed that they filled The Oaks straight away, and I don't know that it's happened yet that there isn't room for someone, but if there were an epidemic, flu or something, they probably couldn't accommodate it. (Bungalow resident, 2000)

> I think one of the problems, whether rightly or wrongly, is they took in too many people at the top end, and I speak as one of them. I probably ought to have been excluded. This has meant there has been a great demand on the care services particularly cleaners …
> (Bungalow resident, 2000)

A few residents had also reported what they thought of as inequity in the allocation of care and support services.

Now we all know there are people who ask from the moment they come in, and are very demanding. And there are others who are very quiet, very able, and don't like to make a fuss and consequently are not going to get the help they need …I feel there is a disparity there that I feel could have been overcome. (Bungalow resident, 2000)

Care staff had in some respects shared some of the concerns reported by residents during 2000. When they were interviewed in 2001, staff recalled the early operation of Hartrigg Oaks as being a period in which services were evolving. They reported that there had been some inconsistency, particularly in the delivery of support and care to the first arrivals at Hartrigg Oaks, before assessment procedures had become established. Staff also reported the important role that rumour, fuelled by some initial inconsistencies, had played in shaping the perceptions of the support and care services among the residents.

Staff recognised that, despite the planning that had gone into the development, it had been difficult to know what to expect when Hartrigg Oaks first opened. It had also been difficult to channel residents' expectations, as both the care and catering services had been stretched to capacity by the arrival of large groups of residents all at once. Staff shared residents' perceptions that there had been an underestimate of the need for 'Home Help'.

Over time, staff felt that care services had been successfully orientated to residents' needs and that expectations were being more carefully directed. This had led to earlier tensions around needs and wants decreasing.

By 2002, many of the concerns raised by residents in 2000 were largely or wholly resolved. There was almost universal acceptance among residents of assessment as the means by which support and care were allocated, and the assessment process within Hartrigg Oaks was generally viewed as both equitable and effective.

Between 2000 and 2002, there had been some organisational changes at Hartrigg Oaks. These included a greater focus on admitting new residents who were generally younger. In addition, a dedicated management post had been created for bungalow care, replacing the original single post that was responsible for all the care services on site. However, perhaps the most important change was that assessment of care and support services was, by 2002, no longer working according to anticipated plans of need among a theoretical population of older people, but had instead become increasingly well tuned to the needs of the Hartrigg Oaks population. This process, in itself, had addressed many of the earlier concerns of bungalow residents.

This was perhaps best evidenced by the way in which Hartrigg Oaks had reorientated itself to provide a significantly higher level of 'Home Help' service than had originally been envisaged. There is increasing evidence of a need among many older people for services like the 'Home Help' offered by Hartrigg Oaks to help them maintain their independence (Clark *et al.*, 1998; Quilgars, 2000; Raynes *et al.*, 2001).

That Hartrigg Oaks was able to reorientate itself fairly rapidly to a position in which it could respond to this need by providing a larger Home Help service was a strong indicator of its success. Home Help quickly became the single largest element of the services delivered to bungalow residents, and the perception of care and support services among bungalow residents became increasingly positive.

Views of services delivered to the bungalows

There were very positive views of the support and care services among those bungalow residents who had used them. Figure 8 shows that almost all those using the Handyman, Home Help, Personal Care and Pop-in service described them as 'good'. Similarly high ratings were reported among those who stayed for short periods in The Oaks. The only service that was viewed less positively was the quality of the meals delivered to bungalows.

Figure 8 Percentage of bungalow residents who had used care and support services rating them as 'good'

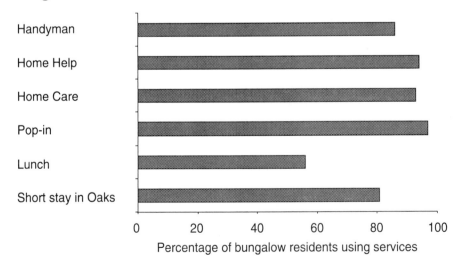

Percentage of bungalow residents using services

Source: 2002 postal survey. Base: those reporting using each service[2]

The findings from the 2000 survey were nearly identical, although at that time the Pop-in service was not yet operational. When interviewed, residents were often full of praise for the care and support services.

It's first class, one hour a week for housework, also someone pops in each morning to see I'm still here. Although it sounds very little, it is of great importance if you're on your own, to know there's someone coming in just to see you, it makes you feel like you belong, and they know you're still here ...
(Bungalow resident, 2000)

We have seen how very well it has worked moving to and fro between The Oaks and the bungalows, and things seem to have worked exactly as we were told it should.
(Bungalow resident, 2000)

The care in the bungalows has been wonderful, absolutely wonderful, they don't fuss but they come and they see how you're getting on, if you want something fine, they'll do their best, if you want to have a natter with them they'll pop in, one occasion I was in bed, they knew I was in bed, one of them came over and said 'look it's the weekend, don't you think you should send for the doctor' and they persuaded me, I'd said 'oh no, I'll be alright', but they persuaded me ... it was just having somebody, when you're on your own ... and yes it was a sensible thing to do ... and things like that meant a heck of a lot, when you are on your own, when you haven't relatives in the vicinity ...
(Bungalow resident, 2002)

About two years ago I had a very bad back and I can't complain, I was very well looked after, I mean I was at home all the time, but I had somebody come in the mornings who asked was I alright, and did I want meals brought over. I never wanted meals brought over because I was hardly eating anything and somebody came over at night to make sure I was alright. I mean quite a few of the neighbours came in to see if I wanted anything, any shopping. That was my only experience, but it was very good.
(Bungalow resident, 2002)

The care staff were singled out for particular praise by some bungalow residents:

... in my case I've had a lot of ill health whilst I've been here and I have been extremely grateful for the help I've had from the carers and those in charge of the carers, extremely grateful, they're not intrusive, but they're there.

> [Staff member] … was so courteous and helpful and kind, without making me feel, you know what I mean, embarrassed or an old lady who's needing help, and I think that's very important.

No criticism of the quality of the support and care services delivered to the bungalows was encountered from those residents who had used these services in either 2000 or 2002.

There were some concerns that immobility or sensory impairment could mean isolation for some bungalow residents and there was some discussion among staff and residents on this issue. Another related concern for a few residents, while the quality of care and support was good, was the loss of independence that could accompany a deterioration in health.

> I've had a lot of care. I have two that come twice a week … and when I came out of hospital I had somebody come to get me up in the morning and to put me to bed at night and they would have brought me meals and all sorts of things like that. The only problem was the timing, they might come to put you to bed at seven o'clock …

While views of short term stays in The Oaks were generally positive, a few of the bungalow residents who had stayed there for a few days or weeks reported some problems from their perspective. Although much progress had been made in relation to allaying initial resident anxieties about access to The Oaks, there was still, in 2002, a concern among a sizeable minority of residents that a short stay space might not be available if they required it. All those who were interviewed who had stayed in The Oaks for short or interim stays praised the quality of the care. A few had felt less comfortable about what they perceived to be the potential for isolation within The Oaks.

> … referring to the care home, if there could just be five or ten minutes, just to sit and natter because these people are sitting there and nodding off all day, if there was somebody popping in, having a coffee or a tea with them … it's broken the day up for them.
> (Bungalow resident interviewed in 2002)

Sources of support and care

Figure 9 shows the sources of support and care being drawn upon by bungalow residents at Hartrigg Oaks.

The extent to which support and care were delivered by Hartrigg Oaks staff is apparent from Figure 9, with 41 per cent of responding bungalow residents reporting receiving support and care from Hartrigg Oaks' own staff. The next largest sources of support were informal, with 23 per cent of respondents being supported by their partner and 12 per cent being supported by their children or other relatives. Eleven per cent of residents reported being helped by their neighbours, although this was found to include only low-level support. Private-sector care delivery was not found within Hartrigg Oaks, but 9 per cent of residents were paying outside contractors for cleaning services.[3]

During the fieldwork, both residents and staff expressed some concerns that there might be insufficient support for carers at Hartrigg Oaks. A few care staff were concerned that carers might, out of a sense of duty, try to take on more than they should in terms of the care of their partner. Staff felt that carers might also try to manage highly challenging needs, particularly the onset of dementia, by themselves. Some residents also felt that there should be more support services for carers.

Figure 9 Sources of support and care being drawn upon (by percentage of bungalow residents)

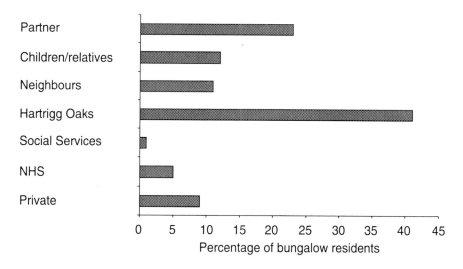

Source: 2002 postal survey. Base: 152 residents

> Quite often they [carers] are desperate before we go in and help them. Because of many things … because they feel it's their duty. But quite often if we're going in one hour a week to do their cleaning we can see where the strains are coming from, and which side they are coming from …
> (Member of care staff, 2001)

> If there was an attractive activity room with occupational therapy in the Care Centre, those that have partners who are caring would have an incentive to go there and give their over-worked partner a break … I think the carer's point of view needs looking at. The person who is ill doesn't realise how much pressure they are putting on the other one.
> (Bungalow resident, 2000)

The results of the 2002 survey of bungalow residents suggested that a quite high proportion of people living with someone else were receiving support from that person. Two out of every five people living with someone else were receiving support or care from that person (44 per cent), while just over one-fifth of people living in a couple were receiving help from Hartrigg Oaks staff (22 per cent).

In contrast, almost two-thirds of bungalow residents who were living alone were receiving at least some support or care from Hartrigg Oaks staff (62 per cent). Overall, people living alone were more likely to be receiving care or support from one or more sources (75 per cent) than people living with someone else (53 per cent).

One statistic did suggest that some of the variation might be partly explained by differences in health status. This was the finding that people living in couples tended to be slightly younger (averaging 76) than those living alone (averaging 80). However, this may not have fully explained the variation in service use between the two groups.

As noted in Chapter 1, Hartrigg Oaks offered two kinds of Community Fee. The standard fee did not increase with the use of care and services made by bungalow residents. 'Fee for care' allowed residents to pay a lower annual charge, but they had to meet the costs of any support or care they used. One-quarter of bungalow residents were 'fee for care' at the start of 2002. There had been a concern within management that they could potentially be deprived of care or support because they lacked the resources to pay for it.

The research did not show lower use of care services by 'fee for care' residents, instead demonstrating that their use of these services was higher than among those bungalow residents paying the standard fee. In both 2000 and 2002, 'fee for care' residents were more likely to be using the Personal Care and Pop-in services. There was also no evidence from the surveys of 'fee for care' residents finding Hartrigg Oaks less affordable than those paying a standard fee.

The Oaks

In 2000, The Oaks residents were largely people who had moved directly there when Hartrigg Oaks had first opened. There had been 14 permanent moves into the 42-room care home from the bungalows over the course of 2001–02.

In both 2000 and 2002, eight out of ten of those Oaks residents who responded to the surveys (who tended to be those residents with better health status), rated the care services they received as either 'good' or 'excellent'. When residents of The Oaks were interviewed, they generally described their care staff as helpful, well trained, patient and friendly.

> First of all I didn't want to [move to The Oaks] a bit, but thinking about it I thought I ought to, but having come it is very good indeed, you see we have nice rooms, as long as one's independent, as I am with this pusher thing, one is well looked after, the staff are very, very good, amazingly patient, helpful and cheerful.
> (Resident of The Oaks, formerly a bungalow resident, 2002)

> And then the staff, incomparable, I can't tell you what I think of them, so thoughtful, so endlessly patient with us, and so thorough, and all do their jobs so inconspicuously, and every journey with a cup of coffee is a sort of friendly look in, and the food! That's important, we have a choice for every meal, including vegetarian, and they look after diets …
> (Resident of The Oaks, 2000)

In both 2000 and 2002, some of the less active residents of The Oaks spoke about isolation and boredom and quite often wanted the care staff to spend more time chatting with them and providing pastoral support.

> Sometimes we like to talk to the carers, but they can't spend any time with us [if] they come in here to have a chat with us, you know, just to make us feel at home. Because otherwise we are sitting here all day long, twiddling our fingers.
> (Resident of The Oaks, 2000)

> We don't see them so often perhaps as we would like, we can be left alone, if we have no interests to take us out or anything, we would like just sometimes a little bit more time, conversation wise …
> (Resident of The Oaks, 2002)

When staff from The Oaks were interviewed in late 2001, they praised the standard of care that was offered and the resources that were available. Those who had worked elsewhere in the care sector compared The Oaks favourably with the other homes that they had worked in. There was some concern that, should a higher proportion of very frail people become resident in The Oaks, the atmosphere that had been created by having a sizeable proportion of residents who were still relatively active would change.

Dementia

The extent to which Hartrigg Oaks could provide a 'home for life' when a resident developed severe dementia-type illness was an issue that arose throughout the research. In early 2003, Hartrigg Oaks was in the process of reviewing options with regard to the on-site care of people with dementia. During the period of the research, a small number of residents with severe dementia-type illnesses were moved off site to NHS services in York.

In both 2000 and 2002, the views of the residents on this subject were found to be mixed. A small number viewed the limitations of dementia care at Hartrigg Oaks as meaning the term 'continuing care community' was a misnomer. Some of this small group wished for JRHT to develop specialised EMI (elderly mentally infirm) services on site.

> … we just assumed that whatever was wrong you would never have to leave … and it's come to the point with dementia that some people have had to leave.

Some residents reported having been quite aware of the limitations of dementia care at Hartrigg Oaks when they moved in. For a few people, usually those who had experienced dementia among their family or friends, dementia care was seen as a highly specialised service, not something that could be provided at Hartrigg Oaks.

> … I never thought that, I mean it was obvious that it [Hartrigg Oaks] couldn't cope with a really disturbed person.

Some residents were concerned that they might have to leave the site if they developed dementia. Couples, in particular, had worries about potential separation.

> I mean, again, that's what we thought, we thought, well, if either of us need to go to a nursing home, even if we're pretty old and the other one's pretty fragile and in the bungalow, nevertheless you're near enough to be able come and see them. So you don't want your other half to be somewhere else later on, you want to die on site sort of thing …

When staff were interviewed in 2001, there were some concerns about the care and support of those bungalow residents who were clearly in the early stages of dementia. It appeared at that time that Hartrigg Oaks was not entirely equipped to provide appropriate services.

> I would say the only people we've not really catered for are the elderly mentally infirm. I would say there was a gap there. They do get help, and they do get looked after, but we don't really cater for them.
> (Member of Hartrigg Oaks staff, 2001)

The 2000 and 2002 fieldwork included some residents whose partners, friends or neighbours had developed dementia. A few were concerned that these individuals had eventually been moved to NHS services. However, many praised the sensitivity of the care staff at Hartrigg Oaks.

> There are one or two people who suffer from that [dementia], but I think it has been handled very sensitively as far as I am aware. What I've observed of the one or two, it's been handled exceptionally well.

Among both residents and staff there was a concern about the management of dementia as the average age of Hartrigg Oaks residents increased. Both the residents and staff who commented on this were mindful of the association between the prevalence of dementia and age. Prevalence rates currently increase substantially with age. While one in 1,000 people aged 40–65 develop a form of dementia, the rate increases to one in 50 by age 65–70 and to one in 20 by age 70–80. One in five people aged over 80 have a form of dementia-type illness.[4]

> As we live longer and longer, it will become more important, I mean it ought to be thought about ... but I think it will become very important in the future, because you can look after a person physically, quite easily, but not mentally ...

Difficulties for some residents in living alongside people with dementia were reported by both staff and residents. Staff reported that one resident with early stage dementia sat alone in the coffee shop as no one would sit with her.

> ... how would they feel if it happened to themselves or somebody they were very close to, how would they cope with it, how would they feel, especially in a community as Hartrigg, and not to feel that the person should be locked away, be taken away from the community, they need as much support, as much communication with others as possible.
> (Member of Hartrigg Oaks staff interviewed in 2001)

Some residents did report more positive attitudes towards other residents who had early stage dementia. This seemed to be particularly the case when someone was in a seemingly benevolent state. Those residents who were in this group were usually referred to as 'wanderers', reflecting their tendency to be out and about within The Oaks Centre.

5 Conclusions

The research design, developed by the Centre for Housing Policy in consultation with JRF and the Project Advisory Group, focused on gaining an understanding of what attracted older people to Hartrigg Oaks and their views on the experience of living there. Beyond these questions, the research also sought to review any lessons that might be applied to the possible replication of the Hartrigg Oaks model. Many aspects of the operation of Hartrigg Oaks, from the logistics of delivering the care services through to the running costs of the community, were not examined by this research.

This study is one part of an ongoing assessment of Hartrigg Oaks that will also include a comparative and evaluative study comparing Hartrigg Oaks with other innovative housing models for older people.

Hartrigg Oaks is designed as a community that may house some of its current residents for many years to come, in some instances for another 20 years or more. The UK's first CCRC is designed to run for decades and may well undergo significant changes over what will be a long operational life. A study of the views of the first residents on their first few years at Hartrigg Oaks cannot represent the last word on the community. The Hartrigg Oaks of 2020 will have evolved and changed to cater for changing resident needs and may be quite different to the community that participated in this research.

The attraction of Hartrigg Oaks for older people

Hartrigg Oaks offered a combination of accommodation and services that was attractive to many older people. Hartrigg Oaks was seen to offer a combination of independence and peace of mind for the future.

Since Hartrigg Oaks would be a community in which residents would continue to live independently, perhaps for many years, factors such as the bungalow design, space standards, privacy, access to amenities on and off site, and the location of the scheme, were as important to prospective residents as they would be to any home buyer seeking a new home. As Chapter 2 showed, the range of care that Hartrigg Oaks offered was a major attraction, but the capacity of the community to address a range of housing and other needs was also a major factor influencing residents' decisions to move.

Although Hartrigg Oaks was seen to be expensive, many residents had carefully considered the financial implications of moving there. Many felt the costs of residence at Hartrigg Oaks compared well with the other alternatives available to them.

Resident satisfaction

What clearly emerges from this study is the inherent attractiveness of the concept of a CCRC, and the high levels of satisfaction among the great majority of residents of Hartrigg Oaks who felt their expectations of what would be on offer had been matched by their experiences. Of course, Hartrigg Oaks is not for everyone. There are those who would never wish to live in housing that was demarcated on the basis of age. Indeed, there were a handful of residents in Hartrigg Oaks who regretted their decision to move there. Nevertheless, there is evidence from this research that Hartrigg Oaks represented a model of living for later life that met the diverse needs of its residents.

The accommodation, care and support services, amenities, range of social activities, site layout and design and many other aspects of life at Hartrigg Oaks were widely praised by residents. Nevertheless, some mistakes were made, with aspects of the bungalow design and in the early organisation and delivery of care services.

There were concerns among some residents and staff, which were supported by some of the research findings, that satisfaction with life at Hartrigg Oaks could be lower for those residents with poorer health. One issue for Hartrigg Oaks is the extent to which it should develop its role in relation to providing social support to its less active residents. This is a difficult question, because residents were attracted by the independence offered by Hartrigg Oaks and were positively against being corralled into organised social activities; at the same time, some less mobile residents would have liked staff to take a more proactive role in the social life of Hartrigg Oaks.

Beyond the sense of security provided by care services being present if needed, one of the key attractions of retirement communities is their potential for offering social support. Hartrigg's residents were attracted by the presence of like-minded people and by the social activities on offer. Overall satisfaction was also strongly linked to participation in social networks both within and outside Hartrigg Oaks. Other research has shown that a key determinant of resident satisfaction in sheltered housing is the extent to which social activities and social support are arranged or provided for residents (Nocon and Pleace, 1999).

The potential to provide a socially supportive and stimulating environment is a key argument in favour of retirement communities over the use of floating care and support delivered to older people in general needs housing. Models like 'extra care' housing for 'fit' and 'frail' older people are currently being promoted by the Department of Health and through the Supporting People programme partly on this basis (ODPM, 2003). In many respects, Hartrigg Oaks is a highly successful example of retirement housing that is also a community and is characterised by the extent and success of social networks involving residents. Yet, at the same time, the experience of some of its residents varied in this regard.

Care and support

The residents' views of care and support services had become almost universally positive by the time of the 2002 fieldwork. Every major element of care and support service delivery was overwhelmingly praised by those residents who had made use of those services.

Given the range of on-site care and support, Hartrigg Oaks was clearly able to provide a home for life for most of its residents. Many among its current residents will not need its residential care services, but those residents who do need residential care (on a short-term or permanent basis) can stay in the community that has become their home.

A question remains, however, over the capacity of current services to care for people with more severe dementia-type illnesses. This difficult question has implications for the ambience, management and costs of living at Hartrigg Oaks. At the time of this research, those residents with severe dementia-type illnesses were cared for off site in NHS specialist dementia facilities. Residents had mixed views about the extent to which dementia care can or should be provided within Hartrigg Oaks. The care of dementia sufferers will also be a key question for any organisation developing new housing, if they either directly follow the Hartrigg Oaks model or develop their own 'Hartrigg-like' model.

Discussion

Hartrigg Oaks is an independent, non-profit-making community, wholly funded through JRHT and the contributions made by its residents. As it requires both a capital investment and a quite substantial annual fee from its residents, Hartrigg Oaks is not, in its current form, an option that is accessible to most older people in the UK.

Yet on the evidence of this research, the Hartrigg Oaks concept clearly appealed to many older people. Most of its residents felt it had delivered on what had been promised. Hartrigg Oaks was the first example of a CCRC in Britain, an experiment in developing a new form of housing for later life, which in most respects had proved to be very successful. This research did not evaluate the actuarial model on which

Hartrigg Oaks was based, nor did it examine the operating costs of the community, both of which are central to any consideration of replicating the Hartrigg Oaks model. Nevertheless, on the basis of resident satisfaction with Hartrigg Oaks and the attractiveness of the concept, there would seem to be scope to develop further CCRCs aimed at older people with similar income levels.

It is to be noted that residents participating in this research, despite Hartrigg Oaks being 'experimental', clearly trusted and were influenced in their decision to move by the Rowntree name and reputation. Understandably, an organisation not seen to be financially viable, sufficiently experienced in care provision or trustworthy would not have attracted the same level of interest or generated confidence in potential residents. This is a potentially important consideration with respect to replication, as there was some distrust of the profit motive of private companies providing supported housing among the residents.

Beyond providing a basis from which further CCRCs can be developed, Hartrigg Oaks has another potentially important role. Clearly, social rented supported housing or shared ownership schemes for older people cannot use an actuarial model like Hartrigg, but they can perhaps draw lessons from the ways in which it provided support, care and accommodation. The high space standards, amenities and range of care services on offer, as well as the operating ethos of Hartrigg Oaks, with its emphasis on enabling and supporting independence, can clearly be drawn upon by retirement communities financed on a different basis. Hartrigg Oaks is a way of meeting housing needs in later life that, on the basis of resident views, is clearly an effective model. This research provides an evidence base that can be drawn upon by other retirement communities to inform their design and operation.

Notes

Chapter 1

1   See http://www.jrf.org.uk/housingandcare/lifetimehomes/default.asp

2   A small number of residents have other financial arrangements (see following footnote and Appendix B).

3   JRHT did, however, provide 11 bursary bungalow places for older people on low incomes from the surrounding village of New Earswick, which is mainly social housing managed by JRHT.

Chapter 2

1   See Appendix A for details of the research methods.

Chapter 3

1   Additional information on the financial arrangements at Hartrigg Oaks can be found in Appendix B.

2   Although known locally as a 'village', New Earswick is, in effect, a suburb of York, located within the city boundaries.

Chapter 4

1   Additional information on the care and support services provided at Hartrigg Oaks can be found in Appendix B.

2   See Appendix B for more information on these services.

3   The research findings did not suggest this was a result of unmet need for Home Help services. Some Hartrigg Oaks residents were simply used to having a cleaner, having employed one throughout their lives.

4   Source: Alzheimer's Society.

References

Appleton, N. (2002) *Planning for the Majority: The Needs and Aspirations of Older People in General Housing*. York: York Publishing Services/JRF

Brenton, M. (1999) *Choice, Autonomy and Mutual Support*. York: York Publishing Services/JRF

Butler, A.W.J., Oldman, C. and Greve, J. (1981) *Sheltered Housing for the Elderly: Policy, Practice and the Consumer*. London: Allen & Unwin

Callaghan, P. and Morrissey, J. (1993) 'Social support and health: a review', *Journal of Advanced Nursing*, Vol. 18, No. 11, pp. 203–13

Clark, H., Dyer, S. and Horwood, J. (1998) *'That Bit of Help': The High Value of Low Level Preventative Services for Older People*. Bristol: Policy Press

Cohen, S. and Wills, T.A. (1985) 'Stress, social support and the buffering hypothesis', *Psychological Bulletin*, Vol. 98, pp. 310–57

Department of Health (2001) *National Service Framework for Older People*. London: Department of Health

Hanson, J. (2001) *From Sheltered Housing to Lifetime Homes: An Inclusive Approach to Housing*. London: UCL

Hasler, J. and Page, D. (1998) *Sheltered Housing is Changing: The Emerging Role of the Warden*. Nottingham: Metropolitan Housing Trust

Neill, J. *et al.* (1988) *A Need for Care*. Aldershot: Gower

Nocon, A. and Pleace, N. (1999) 'Sheltered housing and community care', *Social Policy and Administration*, Vol. 32, No. 2, pp. 164–80

ODPM (2001) *Under-occupation in Social Housing*. London: ODPM

ODPM (2003) *Supporting People: Guide to Accommodation and Support Options for Older People*. London: ODPM

Oldman, C. (1990) *Moving in Old Age: New Directions in Housing Policies*. London: HMSO

Oldman, C. (2000) *Blurring the Boundaries*. York: Joseph Rowntree Foundation

Quilgars, D. (2000) *Low Intensity Support Services*. Bristol: Policy Press

Raynes, N., Temple, B., Glenister, C. and Coulthard, L. (2001) *Quality at Home for Older People: Involving Service Users in Defining Home Care Specifications*. Bristol: Policy Press

Rugg, J. (1999) *Hartrigg Oaks: The Early Development of a Continuing Care Retirement Community 1983–1999*. York: Centre for Housing Policy

Scales J and Scase R, (2000) *Fit and Fifty?* Swindon: Economic and Social Research Council

Sinclair, I. and Williams, J.P. (1990) 'Settings based services', in I. Sinclair, R. Parker, D. Leat and J. Williams (eds) *The Kaleidoscope of Care: A Review Research on Welfare Provision for the Elderly.* London: HMSO

Sturge M, (2000) *Continuing Care Retirement Communities in the UK: Lessons from Hartrigg Oaks.* York: Joseph Rowntree Foundation

Tinker, A., Wright, F. and Zeilig, H. (1995) *Difficult to Let Sheltered Housing.* London: HMSO

Appendix A: Research methods

The research began in the spring of 2000, and was completed in late 2002. Quantitative and qualitative methods were employed including: two postal surveys directed to all residents at Hartrigg Oaks; an extensive series of face-to-face interviews and discussion groups with residents (almost one in three residents participated in elements of the research); face-to-face interviews and discussion groups with members of staff at Hartrigg Oaks and a discussion group with residents from New Earswick.

A small number of contextual interviews were also conducted with local community and primary health care professionals and managers from York City Council Community and Family Services. These interviews provided useful material relating to the development of a CCRC, and the relationship of Hartrigg Oaks with other service providers, and are reported elsewhere.

Data from the surveys were processed, using data entry checking, and collated using Foxpro database management software and analysed with SPSS statistical analysis software.

The research team employed semi-structured interview techniques with both the focus groups and the one-to-one interviews conducted for the research. Semi-structured interviewing techniques enable the interviewee or participants to raise and prioritise the issues they are concerned with. The researcher ensures that the interview covers all the topics that are pertinent to the research, but otherwise takes a passive, rather than leading role.

Interviews were undertaken on the basis that those participating had given what the researcher judged to be informed consent. This meant that participants had to be fully aware of the purpose and nature of the research in which they were engaged, were aware that they did not have to answer any question with which they were uncomfortable and that they could end the interview at any time. All interviews and discussion groups were recorded with the permission of the participants, and transcribed for detailed analysis.

Fieldwork with residents

The fieldwork with residents was undertaken in two phases, the first phase in 2000 and the second in 2002.

The first phase of the fieldwork with residents, undertaken in the spring and summer of 2000, consisted of a postal survey, followed by a series of focus groups and interviews. Every effort was made to ensure that the research was as unobtrusive as possible. Prior to beginning the fieldwork, the research team held three presentations for residents where the purpose of the research was explained, and residents' questions and concerns directly addressed. A leaflet explaining the research was also circulated to all the residents and information was also placed in the Hartrigg Oaks newsletter.

The research team sent survey questionnaires to all the occupied bungalows, totalling 149 out of the 152 bungalows on site. One hundred and thirty-four responses were returned directly to the research team, a response rate of 90 per cent. These 143 bungalows included 43 two-person households, and 91 single-person households. The questionnaires were designed to gather information on the characteristics of both residents in two-person households, and to allow both individuals to express their own opinions. Data from the survey therefore covered 171 individuals. Results of the survey are presented in terms of individual rather than household responses. Responses were anonymous.

A survey questionnaire was also sent to the residents of The Oaks. At that time, 36 out of the 41 rooms were occupied. Twenty-one responses were received, a response rate of 58 per cent. This response rate is low in comparison with the response rate from bungalow residents; however, many of The Oaks residents had health problems that would make completing a questionnaire difficult. Given the frailty of some residents, the research team did not send 'chase-up' letters to non-responders.

The first survey was followed up by a series of interviews and discussion groups with residents. Two semi-structured interview schedules were designed for use in the interviews and discussion groups with bungalow residents and Oaks residents, both consisting of a series of open-ended questions. The questions sought to ascertain residents' views and perceptions of a number of topics: their reasons for moving to Hartrigg Oaks, their views on care services, facilities and amenities on site, the design of the bungalows and the site generally, as well as their perceptions of value-for-money, community development and management issues.

In order to invite the bungalow residents to participate, 90 bungalow addresses were randomly selected. For reasons of confidentiality, the names of the residents living at the selected addresses were not known to the research team. Forty letters were sent asking whether the resident/s would be prepared to take part in a face-to-face interview with a member of the research team; 50 letters asked whether the residents would be prepared to take part in a discussion group. Residents were asked to return a form giving their name, address and telephone number if they wished to participate. No further attempt was made to contact those who did not reply.

Four discussion groups and 27 face-to-face interviews were conducted. A total of 62 bungalow residents took part, representing 53 households or slightly more than one-third of all bungalow households at Hartrigg Oaks. It is to be noted that those residents who took part were a self-selecting sample, and it may be that they differ in some respects from those who did not agree to take part.

It was anticipated that many Oaks residents would not be able to participate in an interview because of poor health. The research team therefore contacted the Head of Care within The Oaks to ask for a list of those residents who, the care staff felt, would not be able to participate in an interview. Of the 36 residents, the Head of Care identified 12 who were in good enough physical and mental health to take part in an interview. The research team approached all 12 residents, however, only four agreed to participate in this element of the research.

The results of the first phase of the fieldwork were reported to residents at a special presentation at Hartrigg Oaks, and an Interim Report placed in the Hartrigg Oaks library.

The second phase of the fieldwork with residents was undertaken in the summer of 2002 and, although broadly similar methodologies (a resident survey, followed by interviews and discussion groups) were employed, there were some modifications. Following the random selection of potential interviewees in 2000, some bungalow residents had objected to being approached in this way. The 2002 survey questionnaires therefore asked bungalow residents and residents of The Oaks to volunteer to take part in either an interview or discussion group.

As before, the bungalow survey questionnaire was designed to allow individuals in two-person households to make their own responses. The survey achieved a response rate of 72 per cent (110 of 152 bungalows), the responses representing 152 individuals. The 2002 survey of residents of The Oaks also had a lower response rate than in 2000, with 19 individuals responding (46 per cent). A total of 58 residents participated in the interviews and discussion groups held in 2002. Twenty-four bungalow residents took part in four discussion groups. As volunteers could be matched to their survey responses, it was possible to compose one of the discussion groups of residents who had arrived relatively recently in the community and another of residents who had participated in the interviews and discussion groups in first phase of the fieldwork. A further 29 bungalow residents and five Oaks residents took part in face-to-face interviews.

Fieldwork with staff

In the summer and autumn of 2001 a series of semi-structured, one-to-one and group interviews was held with staff working at Hartrigg Oaks, and a total of 15 individuals took part. The managers from the three services strands – Home Care, The Oaks and the catering/housekeeping – were interviewed. Other members of the Home Care team, The Oaks care team and catering staff participated in three discussion groups.

The interview schedule asked staff about their perceptions of the CCRC concept and more particularly perceptions about Hartrigg Oaks, the level and quality of services and whether a community was developing. The interviews also covered the relationship between Hartrigg Oaks and New Earswick and about their general experiences of working in the first UK CCRC.

Fieldwork with residents of New Earswick

In the autumn of 2002, a discussion group with residents of New Earswick was arranged. Contact was initially made with the New Earswick Residents Forum, and a meeting with a group of eight residents arranged with the assistance of the Forum.

Appendix B: Hartrigg Oaks monitoring report by the Joseph Rowntree Housing Trust

Residents

The total number of residents at Hartrigg Oaks at the beginning of each year is shown in Table B1.

Table B1 Total population at Hartrigg Oaks, 1999–2003

Year	1999	2000	2001	2002	2003
Total residents	160	195	200	203	205

After full occupancy during 1999, the yearly total has stayed around 200 residents, but is slightly increasing owing to couples' being given priority on vacancies for Hart (two-bedroom) bungalows. Also, as residents take up permanent occupancy in The Oaks, their bungalows are re-let, resulting in an increase in the total population.

The proportion of women to men has increased slightly over the period to 67 per cent female and 33 per cent male. Figure B1 shows this breakdown, based on figures as at 1 January each year.

Figure B1 Gender of Hartrigg Oaks residents

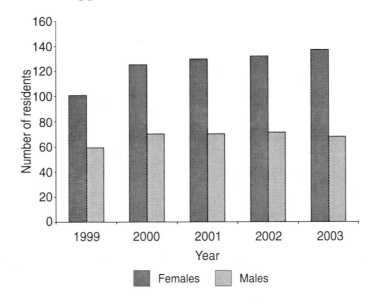

Out of the total population of 205 residents at 1 January 2003, there are 107 single residents (52 per cent) and 98 residents (48 per cent) who are part of a couple. Figure B2 shows the breakdown of households.

Figure B2 Singles and couples – breakdown of households

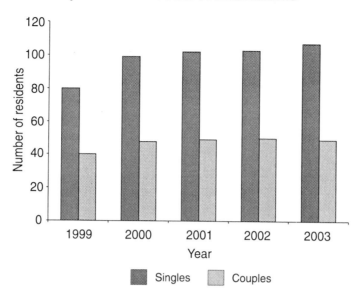

At 1 January 2003, 7 residents who originally came to Hartrigg Oaks as a couple now live alone.

The average age of the population has increased from 76 years to 78 years, as shown in Table B2.

Table B2 Average ages of population

Year	Average age
1999	76 years
2000	77 years 1 month
2001	77 years 7 months
2002	78 years 1 month
2003	78 years 6 months

If the population did not change, the average age would of course increase by one year every 12 months. The fact that the actual increase has been at only half that rate is due to the allocation of vacancies being given in ascending order of age of applicant, subject to a minimum age of 60.

Figure B3 shows the age distribution on a yearly basis.

The youngest members at 31 December 2002 were aged 62 (two residents), and the oldest were aged 95 (bungalow resident) and 97 (Oaks resident).

Figure B3 Age profiles of population

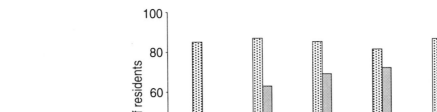

Table B3 shows the numbers of residents who joined and left each year and their average ages.

Table B3 Leavers and joiners – Hartrigg Oaks

	1999			2000			2001			2002	
L	**D**	**J**	**L**	**D**	**J**	**L**	**D**	**J**	**L**	**D**	**J**
1	4	40	1	6	10	3	6	14	1	10	10
69.5	83.6	76.8	73.9	85.8	70.7	79.4	79.4	72.1	81.9	81.9	68.3

L=left; D=died; J=joined

During 2002, ten new residents joined Hartrigg Oaks. This is the same number as in 2000, but less than in 2001.

There have been a total of 26 deaths since 1998 – four during 1999 followed by six in both 2000 and 2001 and ten during 2002.

Since 1999, five residents have left to live elsewhere, one couple and three single people. A further two residents (couple) are set to leave in January 2003.

Since 1999, there had been a total of 17 permanent moves by bungalow residents into The Oaks, of whom seven subsequently died, as shown in Table B4. The average number of weeks spent in The Oaks by permanent residents is 42 weeks.

Table B4 Permanent moves to The Oaks, and subsequent deaths

	1999			2000			2001			2002	
P	**D**	**ALOS**	**P**	**D**	**ALOS**	**P**	**D**	**ALOS**	**P**	**D**	**ALOS**
0	0	0	2	0	135 weeks	5	3	38 weeks	10	4	25 weeks

P=permanent; D=died; ALOS=average length of stay

Bungalow services

This part of the report looks at the delivery of bungalow services to the residents at Hartrigg Oaks. The bungalow care team provides three classifications of services, shown in Table B5.

Table B5 Classification of services

Type of care	Description
Home Help	Vacuuming, dusting, washing up, changing beds, mattress turning, laundry of clothing, bed linen and towels. Basic shopping service for food and cleaning materials
Personal Care	Dressing, undressing, bathing, toileting, meal preparation, assistance with medication
Pop-in	Up to 15 minutes. Emotional support, meal delivery and some lower levels of Personal Care such as toileting or meal preparation.

When a resident is in need of care, a request is made to the Community Care Coordinator for an assessment. Support is available when a resident is unable to carry out a particular activity for him or herself. In the case of couples, if one member is able to carry out an activity, such as Home Help, but not the other member, support would not usually be made available.

Home Help is provided per household as the services are generally of benefit to both residents in a couple. The following sections show Home Help to bungalows and Care Services to Residents. The data are shown each quarter from 1 October 2000, when records commenced on the current basis.

Figure B4 shows the average hours of each type of care that were delivered each week. The table shows that there has been little overall change in the period in the amount or type of services provided, although the distinction between the three categories has been more significant.

Figure B5 shows the average hours per week of care provided to residents.

Figure B4 Average weekly hours of bungalow service

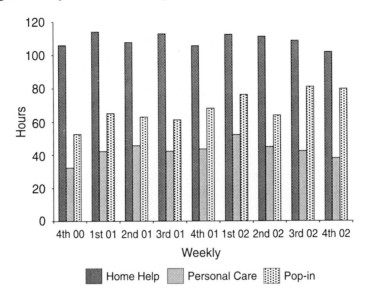

Figure B5 Range of minimum and maximum weekly hours of bungalow services, and average hours per resident

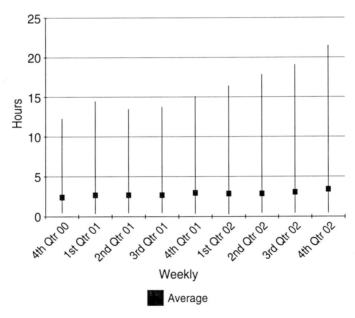

The range of hours of bungalow services has steadily increased. It can be seen that the average per resident is also (slightly) increasing, but that the average is much closer to the minimum hours per resident.

Home Help

The average number of households to receive Home Help each week during each period is shown in Table B6, and has been fairly constant over the period.

Table B6 Average number of households in receipt of Home Help each week

Period	4th Qtr 00	1st Qtr 01	2nd Qtr 01	3rd Qtr 01	4th Qtr 01	1st Qtr 02	2nd Qtr 02	3rd Qtr 02	4th Qtr 02
Average weekly number of households	61	69	67	65	60	64	61	61	56
% of total population (as at 1/1 each year)	30	34	33	32	29	31	30	30	27

The drop in the 4th quarter of each year is as a result of Christmas and New Year, when Home Help hours are reduced where possible to cater for staff holidays over the period.

Figure B6 shows the average range of hours per week of Home Help provided to residents.

Figure B6 Range of weekly hours of Home Help delivered and average per resident

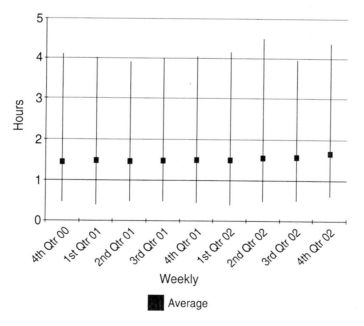

Weekly

■ Average

The average number of hours of Home Help received by residents has ranged over the five year period from 1.3 to 1.7 hours per week.

Most households received no more than two hours per week. However, although the number of households who received more than four hours per week has remained constant, the occurrence of occasions where over four hours of Home Help has been provided has increased sharply from nine occasions up to the end of 2001 to 20 times during 2002. No household received more than six hours per week at any time during the recorded time period.

Personal Care

The average number of residents to receive Personal Care each week during each period has remained stable and is shown in Table B7.

Table B7 Average number of residents in receipt of Personal Care each week

Period	4th Qtr 00	1st Qtr 01	2nd Qtr 01	3rd Qtr 01	4th Qtr 01	1st Qtr 02	2nd Qtr 02	3rd Qtr 02	4th Qtr 02
Average weekly number of residents	14	15	17	17	16	18	17	15	16

There was a broader split in hours of Personal Care as compared with Home Help delivered in the average week. However, most residents still received three hours per week or less. The position is analysed in Table B8.

Table B8 Breakdown of hours per week (average number of residents) of Personal Care

Number of hours per week	4th Qtr 00	1st Qtr 01	2nd Qtr 01	3rd Qtr 01	4th Qtr 01	1st Qtr 02	2nd Qtr 02	3rd Qtr 02	4th Qtr 02
≤3	9	10	12	12	12	14	14	13	15
>3 and ≤6	4	4	3	4	3	2	2	2	1
>6 and ≤9	–	1	1	2	2	1	1	1	0
>9	–	1	1	1	1	1	1	1	1

During 2001 there were two weeks in which more than 12 hours of care were delivered to a single resident. This increased during 2002, where the number of occasions where more than 12 hours of care in a week were delivered to a single resident was one in the first quarter, seven in the second, six in the third and ten in the fourth quarter.

Figure B7 Range of weekly hours of Personal Care and average per resident

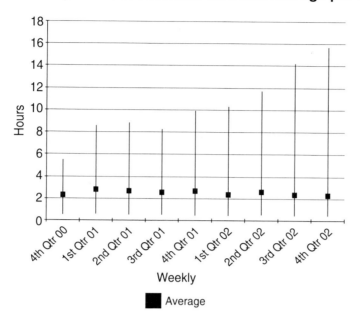

The maximum number of hours of Personal Care delivered to bungalow residents climbed throughout 2002, but the average has slightly dipped (see Figure B7). The increase in the maximum hours was as a result of a higher demand from one resident.

Pop-ins

The average number of residents to receive Pop-ins each year increased slightly during 2002 (see Table B9).

Table B9 Average number of residents in receipt of Pop-ins each week

Period	4th Qtr 00	1st Qtr 01	2nd Qtr 01	3rd Qtr 01	4th Qtr 01	1st Qtr 02	2nd Qtr 02	3rd Qtr 02	4th Qtr 02
Average weekly number of residents	20	23	22	20	24	25	21	27	26

There was a similar split in hours of Pop-ins to Personal Care delivered in the average week. Most residents still received three hours per week or less. The position is analysed in Table B10 and Figure B8.

Table B10 Breakdown of hours per week (average number of residents) of Pop-ins

Number of hours per week	4th Qtr 00	1st Qtr 01	2nd Qtr 01	3rd Qtr 01	4th Qtr 01	1st Qtr 02	2nd Qtr 02	3rd Qtr 02	4th Qtr 02
≤3	14	14	13	10	13	14	13	17	15
>3 and ≤6	6	8	7	8	10	9	7	9	10
>6 and ≤9	–	1	2	2	2	2	2	1	1

Figure B8 Range of weekly hours of Pop-ins delivered and average per resident

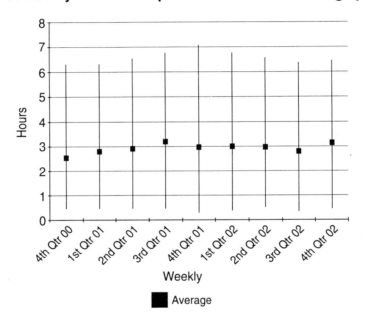

On six occasions during 2001, one resident received more than nine hours of Pop-ins. During 2002, no residents received this level of support.

The Pop-in service also includes the delivery of meals to residents in their bungalows. The position is set out in Table B11.

Table B11 Average meal deliveries each week and number of residents

	4th Qtr 00	1st Qtr 01	2nd Qtr 01	3rd Qtr 01	4th Qtr 01	1st Qtr 02	2nd Qtr 02	3rd Qtr 02	4th Qtr 02
Average number of meals delivered each week	–	26	26	31	40	22	12	18	25
Average number of residents having a meal delivered each week	–	4	4	4	7	2	1	2	2

The Oaks services

This section sets out the use of the residential home The Oaks, which has 42 single rooms. Residents in The Oaks comprise two groups: first, those who come direct to The Oaks on a conventional residential home basis; second, those who come from a Hartrigg Oaks bungalow. The respective numbers for the two groups are set out in Tables B12 and B13.

Table B12 External residents of The Oaks

	1999	2000	2001	2002
At beginning of year (1 January)	33	35	37	32
Admissions	8	5	4	0
Death/hospitalisation	(2)	(3)	(8)	(4)
Moved to another care establishment	(4)	(0)	(1)	(1)
At end of year (31 December)	35	37	32	27

Table B13 Bungalow residents of The Oaks

	1999	2000	2001	2002
At beginning of year (1 January)	1	2	3	10
Short-term admissions	32	37	27	24
Permanent admissions[a]	1	1	8	7
Return to bungalows	(30)	(34)	(26)	(16)
Death/hospitalisation	(1)	(3)	(2)	(9)
Moved to another care establishment	(1)	0	0	(1)
At end of year (31 December)	2	3	10	15

[a] Note: Includes those residents who originally moved to The Oaks on a short-term basis but subsequently became permanent. There has only been one occasion when a resident has moved permanently to The Oaks without a short-term assessment period

The following sections provide further information on the figures for bungalow residents.

The Oaks – short-term stays

The number of bungalow residents requiring short-term care in The Oaks has remained broadly constant over the last three years (see Tables B14 and B15).

Table B14 Average length of bed-nights at The Oaks per resident

	2000	2001	2002
Total number of bed-nights	550	895	674
No. of residents	22	24	23
Average length of stay (bed-nights)	25	37	29

The number of residents takes into account residents who have had more than one stay

Table B15 Source of admissions to The Oaks

Source	2000	2001	2002
Bungalows	30	26	24
Hospital	8	9	7
Other medical establishment	0	0	0

During 2000, the maximum number of stays in The Oaks by a single resident was six. This dropped to three in 2001 and four in 2002.

The Oaks – discharge

Discharges of short-term residents from The Oaks are analysed in Table B16.

Table B16 Discharges of short-term residents from The Oaks[a]

Discharges	2000	2001	2002
Bungalows	33	28	15
Hospital	3	0	2
Permanent	2	5	10
Deceased	0	0	2
Other medical establishment	0	0	1

[a] *Three bungalow residents had not been discharged from The Oaks as at the end of 2002*

Hartrigg Oaks – total services

Table B17 and Figure B9 combine the amount of services provided to residents in bungalows with that provided to residents in The Oaks, both those who transferred permanently and those who received short-term care.

It is interesting to note that, although the average hours of care provided to bungalow residents remained steady during 2002, the hours of care provided to residents in The Oaks increased significantly (by 44 per cent). This would be expected, taking into account the increase in bungalow residents moving permanently into The Oaks and the introduction of younger, healthy residents into the community.

Table B17 Hours of care provided – weekly average

	1999	2000	2001	2002
Bungalow residents	122	170	229	232
Oaks residents	28	59	74	107

Figure B9 Care provided

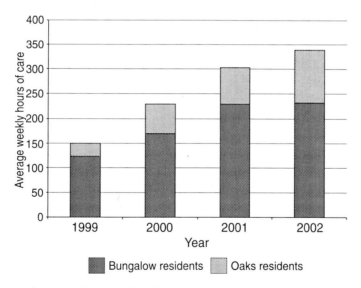

Note: the chart assumes that residents in The Oaks receive 22 hours of care services per week (3.14 per day) and 25 hours (3.57 per day) if the resident is in receipt of nursing care.

Fees

Those living at Hartrigg Oaks pay two fees towards the community's costs.

The Residence Fee

The Residence Fee covers the occupation of a bungalow and use of a room in The Oaks if required. The amount of the fee varies depending on the size and position of the bungalow.

The options are:

(i) Refundable (one-off payment)
   The full fee is repaid – in money, not real terms – to the residents, or their estate, on leaving Hartrigg Oaks on a permanent basis. Repayment is not dependent on selling the bungalow to an incoming resident.

(ii) Non-refundable (one-off payment)
   This fee is lower than the refundable Residence Fee and is based on an individual's age on joining. Partial repayments on a declining basis are made to a resident, or their estate, should they leave within the first 56 months of residence, but no sum thereafter.

(iii) Annualised (monthly payment)
   This annual fee (equivalent to a rent) is calculated from the amount of refundable Residence Fee for each bungalow.

The Community Fee

The Community Fee is payable monthly. It has two components. First, it pays for the running costs of Hartrigg Oaks (such as staffing in the restaurant/coffee shop, repairs and maintenance of bungalows and communal areas, gardening, buildings insurance, administration); and, secondly, it covers the provision of care support, either in a resident's own bungalow or at The Oaks.

The options are:

(i) Standard
   The fees for all residents choosing this option operate on a pooled basis so that the level of the fee is independent of the actual amount of care support which an individual receives. Individuals choosing this option have to meet the JRHT's health check on entry. The fee is related to an individual's age on joining, with a higher fee at older ages.

(ii) Reduced

Individuals may pay an additional non-refundable capital sum on joining Hartrigg Oaks in exchange for a reduced standard Community Fee throughout their period or residence.

(iii) 'fee for care'

If a resident prefers not to participate in the standard arrangement, or if the health criteria at entry are not met, care services are charged for by the JRHT on a pay as you go basis. In addition, these individuals pay a fixed sum each year towards the community's running costs.

Finance

There has been little change by residents in the fee options selected since Hartrigg Oaks opened, as shown in Tables B18 and B19.

Table B18 Residence Fee

Fee type	1998 (as at 31 December)		2002 (as at 31 December)	
	No. of residents	%	No. of residents	%
Fully refundable	96	60	117	57
Non-refundable	45	28	58	28
Mixed fully and non-refundable	8	5	12	6
Bursary	5	3	10	5
Annualised	6	4	8	4

Table B19 Community Fee

Fee type	1998 (as at 31 December)		2002 (as at 31 December)	
	No. of residents	%	No. of residents	%
Standard	94	59	121	59
'fee for care'	48	30	49	24
Reduced	13	8	25	12
Bursary	5	3	10	5

Increases in the Community Fee take place on 1 April each year. Under the terms of the lease with each resident, the maximum increase is 3 per cent above the increase in the index of retail prices in the 12 months to the previous 31 December. Actual increases since 1998 in comparison with the maximum permitted increase is shown in Table B20.

Table B20 Actual increases in Community Fee since 1998

	1 April 1999 (%)	1 April 2000 (%)	1 April 2001 (%)	1 April 2002 (%)	1 April 1998–1 April 2002 (%)
Increase in Community Fee	4.0	4.5	4.5	3.0	17.0
Increase in RPI to previous 31 December	2.8	1.8	2.9	0.7	8.4
Maximum increase of RPI+3%	5.8	4.8	5.9	3.7	21.8

January 2003